George Ashton Black

The History of Municipal Ownership of Land on Manhattan Island

George Ashton Black

The History of Municipal Ownership of Land on Manhattan Island

ISBN/EAN: 9783744725774

Printed in Europe, USA, Canada, Australia, Japan

Cover: Foto ©Suzi / pixelio.de

More available books at **www.hansebooks.com**

STUDIES IN HISTORY, ECONOMICS AND PUBLIC LAW

EDITED BY THE FACULTY OF POLITICAL SCIENCE OF
COLUMBIA UNIVERSITY
IN THE CITY OF NEW YORK

Volume I]   [Number 3

THE HISTORY OF

MUNICIPAL OWNERSHIP OF LAND

ON MANHATTAN ISLAND

To the Beginning of Sales by the Commissioners of the
Sinking Fund in 1844

BY

GEORGE ASHTON BLACK, PH.D.

Second Edition

COLUMBIA UNIVERSITY
New York
1897

TABLE OF CONTENTS

PAGE

INTRODUCTION 9

CHAPTER I

ESTATE GRANTED BY APOSTILE OF 1658 12

Incorporation of New Amsterdam—Slender fiscal powers of the corporation—Grant of city hall—Division line between boweries and incorporated town—The burgomasters allowed to distribute lots—Ordinance concerning lots held vacant—Unconceded lots granted to the city—Extension of city limits under first English governor—The new corporation succeeds to the property rights of the old—Estimate of the estate received in 1658.

CHAPTER II

ESTATE GRANTED BY THE CHARTER OF 1686 17

1. 1686–1733

Water lot grants in fee, and sale of isolated outlying upland 17

Reservations in Dongan Charter—Beginnings of municipal taxation—Special assessments for special benefit—Minister's and poor's rate—Law of 1701—Occasional imposition of a city rate by special act of Assembly—Sales of water lots to pay fees for charter—And to pay for ferry and market houses—First transfer of city land to any church or institution—Defense loan and sales—New city hall—Location of the commons—Jacob De Key's land—Other sales—Lease of land claimed by Harlem freeholders—Income and expenditure of the corporation from 1704 to 1732—Effect of the Cornbury charter on the ferry revenue—Contest between individuals and the corporation for the privilege of gaining ground from the rivers leads to Montgomery charter—Sales to pay cost of obtaining charter—Beekman's swamp.

2. 1734–1775

Fixed annual quit rents reserved in granting water lots.   Upland leased. 29

Corporation revenue and expenditures, 1734-1750—Beginnings of heavy expense for the poor—Slow growth of the city—Lottery and loan systems entered on to pay for public improvements—Growth of water lot quit-rents—The city rate, hitherto occasionally applied for, now applied for annually—Effect of the revolution on the minister's and poor's rate—First division of corporation upland into building lots—How leased—Upper commons staked out—More grants to churches—End of controversy with Harlem freeholders—Disposition of Harlem commons.

3. 1784–1802

Policy of leasing building lots continued, but one half of upper commons sold in fee **35**

City debt at close of revolution—Back rents—A few sales to meet current needs—Sales of farm land at auction to discharge accrued debt —Extent of such land—Private sale of fifty acres—Extraordinary growth of city between 1790 and 1800—First survey of upper commons into city blocks—Large sales of alternate blocks at auction—Speculative *versus* farm values—Many blocks not claimed, and resold at a discount —Additional private sales—City debt in 1800.

4. 1803–1815

Extensive permanent improvements paid for by the sales of new building lots. Upper commons and most of old building lots leased . . .   **41**

Falling in of lower commons leases — Their number — How renewed—Advance in rents—The future of the city as viewed in 1805— The Inclenberg lots—City hall and Canal street undertakings—The Dove lots—Filling up the Fresh Water—Sale of Barclay, Powder house, and Peck Slip lots—Increase of city debt—Expenditure for Bellevue establishment and city hall leads to sale of half the Collect lots, the old city hall and Hudson market sites, and some Chambers street lots—First city stock issued—Lessees adjudged to pay a share of assessments— Comptroller's plan for a sinking fund—Revenues he would appropriate to it—Forecast of its accumulation—His plan adopted—Sale of Government house property—Commutation of all upland quit-rents allowed, and proceeds appropriated to sinking fund.

5. 1816–1821

Repetition of former experience of sales after war as to down-town lots, but residue of upper commons still under lease **50**

Financial difficulties of 1816–1819—Era of low taxation—Remaining Collect lots, more Chambers street lots and valuable Albany and Varick basins lots sold—Acquisition of Fulton market—Stock of 1820–1821.

6. 1822–1843

Steady conservation of remaining municipal land, with restraint of debt till 1834, after which expenditure on the Croton Aqueduct prepares the way for the policy of 1844   53

Extent of upper commons reserve—Changes in it since sales of 1796 and 1801—General falling in for the second time of down-town leases—Second advance in rents—All proceeds of sales and commutations of all quit-rents appropriated to sinking fund—Amount of sinking fund as compared with the estimate of 1812—Maturing of the stock of 1812—Means adopted to redeem it—State's prison lots—Removal of Bellevue establishment to Blackwell's Island—Purchase of Long Island farms—Effect of opening Erie and Champlain canals—Opening of new streets and avenues through upper commons—The Croton Aqueduct—Minor improvements and acquisitions—The ordinance of 1844—Amount of corporation land given into the control of the sinking fund commissioners—Power over it still remaining to the common council—Policy of the commissioners.

CHAPTER III

ENCROACHMENTS 65

CHAPTER IV

GRANTS TO INSTITUTIONS AND CORPORATIONS 70

CHAPTER V

COMMENT AND CONTROVERSY 74

APPENDIX

a. TABLES 80

b. MAPS 83

THE HISTORY OF

MUNICIPAL OWNERSHIP OF LAND

ON MANHATTAN ISLAND

INTRODUCTION

THE distinction between land reserved for purposes of municipal administration and land held or disposed of solely for
municipal revenue, came necessarily into question for New
York City under the ordinance of 1844, which authorized the
commissioners of the sinking fund to sell and dispose of all
real estate belonging to the corporation and not in use for, or
reserved for, public purposes. Under that ordinance the
courts have held real estate for "public purposes" to be such
as "parks, squares, courthouses, almshouses, engine houses,
penitentiaries and other grounds and buildings of that nature
having a general city character and devoted to general city
uses other than mere revenue,"[1] also markets and wharves.[2]

Since 1686, when, by the Dongan Charter, the city received
most of its primitive estate, the development of the municipality has included an ever better provision for public secur-
ity, health, transit and education; and as a matter of course,

---

[1] Arkenburgh *vs.* Wood, 23 Barbour, 360.

[2] Gerard, *City Water Rights, Streets and Real Estate*, p. 114.

more and more real estate "for public purposes" has been
needed and acquired. In great contrast with this continued
acquisition stands the account as regards municipal real estate
available for mere revenue.[1] It is now more than a generation
since substantially the last of the common lands thus available
were transmuted into private property. It might therefore
seem at first sight of little use to investigate their history.
Nevertheless there is much in the New York of to-day and in
its administration which is referable to the city's ownership of
these lands, or requires for its adequate explanation a knowl-
edge of the circumstances of that ownership. Our numerous
charitable institutions, which are not infrequently regarded as a
proof of an exceptionally active private benevolence, rest in a
large number of cases on endowments of common land; and
not a few well-known family fortunes are traceable to early
purchases from the city. The odd massing and juxtaposition
of public and private institutions which cover almost solidly
seven out of the eight blocks between 65th and 69th streets, Third
and Fourth Avenues, is referable to an exceptionally long-con-
tinued reservation of common land there.[2] The plan of the

[1] From tables A, B and C, appended, it appears that corporation real estate
available for purposes of mere revenue constituted in 1820, nineteen per cent. in
value of all corporation real estate; in 1846, ten per cent.; and in 1855, six per
cent. Also that corporation real estate reserved for public purposes constituted in
1820, five per cent. in value of all real estate public and private; in 1846, eleven
per cent.; and in 1855, eleven per cent.

[2] The list is as follows: 1. City Normal College. 2. Foundling Asylum, R. C.
3. Hahnemann Hospital. 4. Baptist Home. 5. Institution for the Improved Instruction of Deaf Mutes. 6. Public School No. 76. 7. Mount Sinai Hospital
Dispensary. 8. Police Station, 25th precinct. 9. Fire Department Building.
10. Synagogue. 11. Seventh Regiment Armory. 12. Mt. Sinai Hospital. 13.
Chapin Home. 14. Dominican Sisters. 15. St. Vincent Ferrer's Church, Con-
vent and School.

The tract used to be known as the Dove Lots, from the Dove Tavern on the old
post road. See Map VI. and subsequent reference herein. Nos. 10, 14, 15 are
built on ground which the city sold at auction in 1850 and 1885. Nos. 2, 3, 4, 5,
12 and 13 on ground leased of the city for ninety-nine years from 1870 and 1871
at a nominal rent. No. 7 pays the city six hundred and thirty dollars annual rent
for twenty-one years from 1881. The rest are public property.

present streets and avenues, except at either end of the island, was already determined in its main features, for the commissioners who devised it, by the survey of 1796, which first mapped out the bulk of the commons into city blocks.

A more scientific interest attaches to these lands in their relation to the city's financial administration. The clearness and completeness with which their history can be traced in our municipal records since 1686 raises the presumption that an account of them and of the conditions and administrative policy which led to their disposal will be of value as affording additional data to that department of the science of finance which deals with public, especially municipal, land ownership. Such an account is aimed at in the following pages. No large tract has been omitted as distinct from isolated individual lots, and the water lots also are deemed a part of the subject until the adoption of a distinct policy in regard to them in 1734. Involved in the narrative and subordinate to its purpose will be found an account of the city debt up to 1830, with here and there a notice of some peculiar feature of early local taxation.[1]

---

[1] It is much to be wished that a connected description existed of the city's experience in each instance with its other important sources of revenue, whether water lots, docks, ferries, markets or Croton works. The field is inviting to those who would undertake original investigation in the department of municipal administration ; but there is the drawback that up to May, 1831, the records are in manuscript only, and so have to be studied at the city hall. Previous to 1831 the organization of the city government was extremely simple, and the records of a single body, the burgomasters and schepens under the Dutch, the mayor and aldermen thereafter, contain an account of the entire municipal administration. The work which is now intrusted to separate departments, each with its own records, was then done by committees who reported at the meetings of the board, on whose minutes their reports generally appear. It seems strange that records of such scope and value should remain so long unprinted. Their publication was begun during the Tweed regime, and suspended when that fell. A manuscript copy is now in preparation under the direction of the clerk of the common council. With his courteous permission, I have examined these records *seriatim*, and most of the statements of fact which I make are derived from them.

CHAPTER I

ESTATE GRANTED BY APOSTILE OF 1658

As a corporate body the city dates from February 2d, 1653,[1] and starts under the title of " schout, burgomasters and schepens of New Amsterdam."[2] The schout or sheriff was for a short time also the "fiscal" of the West India Company, which still owned most of the island and exercised over it and the rest of the New Netherlands complete governmental powers through director general Stuyvesant and his Council of Five.

The two burgomasters transacted all the financial business of the corporation, and might likewise be members of the Council of Five. The municipal powers granted to them and the five schepens were extremely limited, and in fiscal matters particularly were conferred grudgingly and one by one, as the result of oft-repeated petitions to the director general and the home company. Nearly a year passed before the burgomasters succeeded in getting any fiscal powers at all; and then the grant of a tavern excise, to which a general burgher excise and then a tapster's excise were soon after added, was coupled with the condition, never fulfilled, of paying the salaries of the two preachers, the school-masters and the city secretary. These excises, moreover, were revocable at the will of the director general, who at one time sharply rebukes the city authorities for presuming to ask that they be made permanent. In July, 1654, the city obtained its first piece of real estate, on condition that it should not be sold or mortgaged. This

[1] The records show that on this day the first city officials received their commissions.

[2] Their minutes were translated by Dr. O'Callaghan under a common council resolution of Dec. 20, 1847.

was the Company's tavern by the water side, on the present
Pearl street, at the head of Coenties slip,[1] to be used as a
Stadt Huys, or City Hall. Up to this time the most important work performed under the direction of the municipality
was the erection of a line of palisades across the island along
the line of the present Wall street, north of which were the
outlying boweries or farms, as distinct from the incorporated
town. To pay the city's share of the debt thus incurred, a
special tax of six thousand florins was levied by authority of
the governor general. The tax list numbers two hundred and
twenty-eight names and indicates a population of hardly more
than one thousand.

In September 1655 the dreaded Indian outbreak occurred,
and all outlying settlers left alive were driven for the time being within the wall. Many of the refugees, desiring to remain
permanently, asked that lots be given them for homes within
the city limits, and the burgomasters petitioned the governor
general for a survey in order that the request might be com-
plied with. The survey was ordered " without regard to persons, gardens, or places," and the lots which trenched on land
already disposed of were appraised. The distribution of these
lots, which was to be made on payment where appraised, so as
to recompense former owners, otherwise only on condition that
the recipient build, was intrusted to the burgomasters. A few
months later, the director general deeded to them in their official capacity certain lots west of Broadway, as appears from
a series of five deeds by the burgomasters, all dated August
25th, 1656, in which his deed to them is cited. These lots have
been approximately mapped out by Hoffman,[2] as fronting one
hundred and seventy-six feet on Broadway, beginning about
one hundred and sixty feet south of Rector street and extending west to high water mark.

[1] Map I.

[2] *Estate and Rights of the Corporation of the City of New York*, vol. ii., Dia-
gram I. It is impossible to reconcile known distances with any fixed number of feet

The result of leaving the distribution of the vacant lots to the burgomasters was not entirely satisfactory to the director general. He complains of the "spaciousness and great size of the lots which some hold and occupy, the one more than the other." Two years after the survey just mentioned, he caused a new survey to be made of all the vacant lots, and discovered several hundred within the city wall on which no buildings whatever had been erected. All such lots he ordered to be taxed the fifteenth penny, and the proceeds to be applied to the fortifications. The option was given the owners to pay the tax on a valuation fixed by the burgomasters, or surrender the lots at the same valuation. If the proprietor preferred to fix the valuation himself, the burgomasters were to have a corresponding option either to receive the tax, or to take the lots and convey them at the same price to others, "until they or the proprietors shall construct buildings, when the tax shall cease."

Meanwhile the burgomasters, watchful for ways and means to eke out the scanty revenue of the city, and successful in securing some minor privileges,[1] had petitioned for the unconceded lots within the city walls. On January 20th, 1658, the desired apostile was signed. To just what extent the city benefited and how large a property it thus secured, I have not discovered. Records of the separate proceedings of the burgomasters occur in the same volume with the continuous records of the burgomasters and schepens, but only from March, 1657 to January, 1661. In these a few sales are noted and then in April, 1658 it is resolved to proceed no further with the granting of lots before a map thereof be made. At

to the Dutch rod as used in the old grants. In some grants the rod is defined as of 12 feet, in some as of 13, in some as a Rhineland rod, and in others it is used without definition. Hoffman, vol. li., p. 167. By measuring off the distances given by Hoffman and in the deeds on Lyne's map of 1728, the earliest that is accurate, this and other parcels may be located with some approach to exactness. See Map I.

[1] *Records of Burgomasters and Schepens*, vol. iii., p. 38 of the translation.

this point the entries relative to the sale of lots cease and the map, if it was made, is lost. There are also "Records of deeds and conveyances in New Amsterdam from 1654 to 1672," in the office of the city clerk, but only three or four inconsiderable grants by the burgomasters, beyond the grant of the five lots in 1656, are discoverable. The Albany records may contain others.

On June 12th, 1665, the city was incorporated under English rule by Governor Nichols. His commission to the Mayor, Alderman and Sheriff, constitutes the "inhabitants of New York, New Harlem, with all other his majesty's subjects upon the island called and known by the name of Manhattan's island, one body politique or corporate." Thus the city limits passed Wall street and took in the whole island. One of the "deeds and conveyances" just referred to is interesting because it is expressly stated to be confirmatory of a grant by the burgomasters, and is made by the deputy mayor "under commission and authority given unto us by the Right Hon. Richard Nichols, Esq., Gov."

The inference that the new mayor, aldermen and sheriff stepped immediately into the property rights of the schout, burgomasters and schepens, is confirmed by later proceedings of the "court," as the burgomasters and schepens and after them the mayor and aldermen were called, from the prominence of their judicial functions. Thus in 1671 the court directs a petitioner to make an inquiry "whether there be any lot undisposed of within the city which can be no prejudice to the town or fort;" and the next year allows her "two hundred gilders" in lieu of the lot they have promised her. Governor Lovelace also writes to the court desiring that a gore of land near the fort be given to him and his neighbors at a proper valuation, and the court appoints three men to adjudge the value. Finally Governor Andros in his proclamation of 1675, shortly after the final surrender to the English, formally confirmed all prior grants, concessions and estates.[1]

[1] Gerard, p. 30.

Still there are no data, unless among the deeds or patents recorded in the office of the Secretary of State at Albany, from which it can be gathered what the city's possessions during this time and until the Dongan Charter amounted to, or what benefit the city derived from them. The extent of the original ground briefs [1] from the West India Company to private individuals before the apostile shows that the estate received under it by the city in 1658 could not have been large, and of this, apparently, there remained in 1671 only lots exceptional in their nature or that could not be granted without prejudice to the town or fort. Such, for instance, was the first burial-groud on Broadway, two hundred feet south of the five lots and a little north of the present Morris street,[2] which in 1676 was ordered to be laid out in four lots of twenty-five feet front each, " the same to be sold at a vandoue or outcry."

[1] The descriptive portions of these ground briefs below the wall are quoted by Valentine, *City Manual 1857*, p. 498. The map he gives is not claimed to be accurate, but the total area can be deduced more exactly.

[2] Map I.

CHAPTER II

ESTATE GRANTED BY CHARTER OF 1686

1. 1686–1733

WATER LOT GRANTS IN FEE AND SALE OF ISOLATED OUTLYING UPLAND

FOLLOWING the example of the Dutch Burgomasters twenty-five years previous, and with some experience themselves of the convenience of a source of revenue independent of the governor and council, the mayor and aldermen, soon after the arrival of Governor Dongan, petitioned for the unappropriated lands upon the island to low water mark. Unsuccessful at the time, they subsequently secured this and other concessions in the very liberal Dongan Charter of 1686. The only exceptions from the grant to the city of all such unpatented lands were the following:

Fort James.[1]

One messuage or tenement next the city hall.

One messuage by the fort.

The governor's garden; later known as the queen's garden.

The king's farm.[2]

The swamp next to the king's farm by the fresh water.[3]

The charter gave no right to the corporation to raise money by taxation. The first permanent taxing power which the city

[1] Map I.

[2] Southern portion shown on Map I. The farm and garden were granted to Trinity church in 1705, by letters patent from Governor Cornbury, in the name of Queen Anne. Hoffman, Vol. ii., pp. 175 and 180.

[3] A pond north of the common. Map I.

obtained was to levy special assessments, under an act of 1691, "upon all houses within the said city in proportion to the benefit they shall receive thereby, for and towards the making, cutting, altering, enlarging, amending, cleaning, and scouring all and singular the said vaults, drains, sewers, pavements, and pitchings aforesaid." The act of 1693 for settling a ministry provided that ten vestrymen and two church wardens be chosen annually by the freeholders, the same as the aldermen, and required that the English minister be paid one hundred pounds which should be raised, together with a reasonable amount for the maintenance of the poor, by a tax levied annually, but by the vestry, not by the corporation.[1]

An act of 1701, for appointing more effectual means for defraying the public and necessary charge in each city and county and for maintaining the poor, expressly excepts New York city and Albany, as having their own ways and means for defraying their public charge and maintaining their poor. It does authorize them "upon want of money in the treasury" to lay an annual tax not exceeding three hundred pounds for their public charge, but this provision was not acted upon by New York city, whether because of the three hundred pound limit, or because of the qualification "upon want of money in the treasury;" and the following year special two-year tax laws were obtained, the one "for the better support

[1] In England the act of 1601 transferred the levying of this tax to civil officers. In New York city the vestry retained its powers till the rate disappeared in the revolution. In England, as the expense of local government increased, taxes for other purposes were added to the poor rate and levied on the same basis, for example, the highway rate, the watching rate and the constables' rate, until in 1843 there were already twenty-five such rates tacked on ; so that what was originally a voluntary charitable payment by parishioners to the church officers became the basis of all local taxation. In New York city there were likewise additions for other purposes, yet to be noted, but the system was supplemented by the system of special assessments for special benefit. In England such assessment has only lately been proposed, and meets with bitter opposition. It is also rarely resorted to on the Continent, but its more frequent application is beginning to be advocated. See Friedberg, *Die Besteuerung der Gemeinden.*

of the poor," the other for "public and necessary charges."
Only three times, however, in the next fifty years do these
specially voted city rates occur, the ministers' and poor's rate
and assessment under the act of 1691 constituting the
only local taxation.

The new charter cost the city three hundred and twenty-four
pounds in fees to the governor and his secretary. Roberts
remarks concerning this and a similar expense incurred the
same year by the city of Albany for its charter, that these
charges created no scandal and were accounted the proper
perquisites of the office.[1]   Nevertheless the cost was a matter
of some concern to the city, whose whole annual expenditure
did not equal this amount.[2]   The most convenient resource
was to sell some of the property acquired by the charter; and
this the mayor was appointed to do. Sixteen acres on the
Hudson near the present Gansevoort street were sold to a
neighboring proprietor for sixteen pounds.[3]   Fourteen lots
fronting Dock street, eighty feet deep into the dock as it then
existed,[4] brought four hundred and seventy pounds, as appears
from the mayor's report, or something more than one pound
the front foot for the space between the bridge into the dock,
now Moore street, and the city hall at the head of what is
now Coenties slip.

There was at this time a ready market for the lots along the
east shore as far as Beekman's slip between the lines of high
and low water, marked by the present Pearl and Water
streets,[5] and when the treasurer's statement at the beginning
of 1687 disclosed a still existing debt of four hundred and

[1] *History of New York*, Vol. i., p. 195.

[2] *Valentine's Manual for 1859*, Article on the Financial History of New York
City, from which a number of statistics hereinafter given are taken.

[3] Book A of Grants, in Comptroller's office.

[4] In Map I., eighty feet in depth of Blocks L and M.

[5] Map I.

thirty-four pounds, the corporation[1] did not hesitate to take advantage of the demand.

Eleven of these water lots, extending from the present Coenties slip to Old slip, though not covering the whole space between high and low water,[2] brought as the mayor reports two hundred and ninety-four pounds, very nearly fifteen shillings the front foot.

No further sales of any account were made till after the regime of Leisler, except in 1690, when the city received fifty-five pounds for the vacant yard in the rear of the city hall. After Leisler's death in the spring of 1691, the buyers of the lots formerly sold were pressed to build the street and wharf agreed upon in front of them, and the extension of Broad street by the city between the two blocks sold in 1686 had therefore to be made. It was determined to build a new market house there, and a new ferry house at Peck slip was to be paid for.[3] The revenue of the city, derived chiefly from the ferry and dock,[4] being barely sufficient for its ordinary expenses, any public enterprises of the nature referred to were sure to result in sales of city land. Application to the Assembly for leave to levy a rate additional to the ministers' and poor's rate, as has been stated, was exceptional, the citizens feeling already overburdened by provincial taxes. These were largely a military necessity, due to a frontier open to Canada by easy water communication, and consequent conflicts which checked the growth of the province till after the fall of Quebec. Under such circumstances the space between the eighty feet lots first sold and Water street[5] was disposed of in the autumn of 1691, the city receiving therefor three hundred and ninety-

---

[1] Named in the new charter " The Mayor, Aldermen and Commonalty."

[2] Map I., ninety-five feet in depth of Block N.

[3] Cost £297.   Treasurer's books.

[4] In 1692 the ferry was leased for seven years at the rate of £148 per annum. In 1694 the dock was leased for seven years at £40 per annum.   City Treasurer's books.

[5] The rest of Blocks L and M, on Map I.

seven pounds, according to the deeds in the Comptroller's office.

At the same time the lots between high and low water from Wall street to Beekman's slip[1] were ordered to be exposed for sale. Some of them were claimed by the owners of the adjacent upland, but on summons to produce their patent the claimants could show no right beyond high water mark, and another order of sale was made at the following rates: from Wall street to Maiden Lane[2] twenty-five shillings per front foot; from Maiden Lane to John street, eighteen shillings per foot;[3] and from John street to Beekman slip fifteen shillings per foot.[4] So at these rates, with the condition that Water street be continued thirty feet wide and kept in repair, these lots were sold to any one, after pre-emption offered to the holders of the adjacent upland. The amount obtained, as shown by the report of August 5th, 1692, was five hundred and ninety-four pounds.

A little later a building lot of one hundred and eighty feet front on Garden street and eighty-four feet deep, part of an old city burial ground as old deeds show, which must have been laid out on the abandonment of the first burial ground on lower Broadway as early as 1656, was also sold to the Dutch church, subject to be used for a church or houses for pious and charitable uses. The price agreed upon was one hundred and eighty pieces of eight, or fifty-four pounds, to be paid on sealing the patents, which were delivered February 19th, 1692. Except the gift of a church site to the English church, this is the first transfer of city land to any church or institution.[5] The next was in 1703, when the English church received without cost the new burial place fronting three hundred and ten feet on Broadway,[6] and on a portion of which its

[1] Blocks O, P, Q, R.   Map I.
[2] Blocks O and P.
[3] Block Q.
[4] Block R.
[5] No. 2 on Map I. indicates the building.
[6] Map I.

first church had already been erected, conditioned "forever
after to be appropriated for part of the public church yard
of Trinity church and a burial place for any of the inhabitants of the said city."

In 1694 the citizens had to submit on the order of the governor to a special tax of three pence on the pound for the con-
struction of a battery on the rocks edging the southern point
of the island, and the corporation was obliged to borrow two
hundred pounds on a mortgage of the ferry for like purposes
of defence.[1]   To pay this debt the mayor proposed to sell lots
between Old slip and Wall street.   Here again some of the
upland owners urged a claim to low water mark, but failed to
substantiate it.   A front of two hundred feet[2] was sold, the
price being fixed at thirty shillings the front foot.   Only two
other lots were sold till 1697, when on petition of the purchasers of the ninety-five foot lots between Coenties slip and Old
slip[3] the remaining space of Water street was granted them at
ninepence the square foot.

Between 1696 and 1700 a new ferry-house at Brooklyn and
a new city hall where the sub-treasury now stands at the head
of Broad street[4] were completed.   The cost of the ferry-house
was four hundred and thirty-five pounds.   The city hall was
for the time ambitious and expensive, costing from three thousand to four thousand pounds, as Valentine gives it.   Towards
this amount the old city hall brought nine hundred and twenty
pounds in 1699, and sixteen hundred pounds were raised the
next year by a direct tax under the Act of 1699, which authorized an annual levy for the purpose for three years.   Nevertheless, in 1701 a debt still remained, and to obtain the money
to pay it land sales were resumed.   Hitherto no large tract of
the commons had been parted with except an isolated tract of

[1] These data are from Valentine's article.
[2] Map I., two hundred feet front of Block S.
[3] Block N.
[4] Map I., 3.

sixteen acres on the Hudson. There was but one other large
tract remaining on either river above high-water mark. It lay
between the Harlem line and the Hudson, to the north of
Theunis Ides' land, extending from the present One hundred
and seventh to One hundred and twenty-fifth street, and comprised about two hundred and forty acres. It is shown on the
map which accompanies Riker's history of Harlem as Jacob De
Key's land.[1] As far north as Twenty-eighth street the exceptions from the Dongan Charter, with the patents issued to
private individuals prior thereto, covered practically all the land
above high-water mark save the sixteen acres, certain swamps
and the old Dutch common in the vicinity of the present city
hall. Above Twenty-eighth street to the Harlem line, which
ran due north and south across the island from Seventy-fourth
to One hundred and thirtieth street, as shown on Riker's map,
a single tier of patents stretched from either river a definite distance back into the woods leaving a large core of unappropriated
land in the then wild and inaccessible center of the island, which
passed to the city under the Dongan Charter. One gap along
the river was left into which the city also stepped, the two
hundred and forty acres already described. This tract was
sold at public auction in 1701. The purchaser assigned his
title to Jacob DeKey, to whom the deed was issued in consideration of two hundred and thirty-seven pounds. The
same year, and for a like reason, the ground belong to the
city from high to low-water mark, beginning at Beekman's
slip and running along the strand to the ground of Richard
Sackett, was exposed to sale, and also the narrow strip of upland in part adjoining thereto from Peck's slip to Sackett's,
between the road and the river.[2] Twenty-five lots of twenty-
five feet front were disposed of at the time for five hundred and
fifty pounds, besides the more remote lots fronting Sackett's
land, comprising five hundred and sixty feet front, which were

[1] Map II.

[2] Map I., Blocks T, T, T, and U.

sold to him for ninety pounds.[1] In 1699, a grant had been made to the widow of Leisler, of the unsold portion of block S., namely, about two hundred and twenty-five feet in length eastward from Old slip " in consideration for two streets run through her ground, for which she has had no satisfaction."

After this and the sales of 1701, there remained out of all the space between high and low water from Whitehall to the end of Cherry street at the swamp meadow as shown on Lyne's map, only two hundred and fifty-seven front feet outside street lines, and a corporation lot on the west corner of Peck slip and Water street, fifty-seven feet front by fifty feet deep.

On the Hudson water lots were very little in demand prior to 1734, shippers preferring the East river as more free from ice and freshets. Lyne's map of 1728, therefore, shows the original line of upland except for five hundred and fifty feet granted to four petitioners in 1699. In three of these grants the only consideration was the leveling of the river bank so as to make the streets accessible, and the laying of a wharf. For the fourth grant of three hundred feet, twenty pounds additional were obtained.

The next deficiency of municipal revenue was met by taxation under the two year act of 1702. Three hundred pounds sufficed in 1703, or less than three dollars in the thousand of valuation, and this was reduced to two hundred pounds the next year, since the close of the French war permitted a reduction of the city watch to a peace footing. In this year, 1704, a beginning was made of leasing outlying lands, petitions to purchase having been rejected. Twenty-one year leases were given of Beekman's swamp,[2] and of sixty acres which are readily located on Riker's map from the words of the resolution to lease, when once the point of beginning is ascertained, as it may be from the data given in Tuttle's work.[3] The

[1] Map I., Block V.

[2] Map I.

[3] Abstract of Farm Titles in the City of New York.

sixty acres are thus found to take in nearly all the land included within the extension of the line between the Young
and Bennew patents, the road, and the Harlem line as shown
on Riker's map.[1] The lease is here particularly noted as the
first assertion of the right of the city against the conflicting
right of commonage of the Harlem freeholders.

Their patent issued by Nichols in 1666 fixes the Harlem
line with precision, but adds an undefined right of commonage
in these words: "It is likewise further confirmed and granted
that the inhabitants of the said town shall have liberty for the
conveniency of more range of their horses and cattle, to go
further west into the woods beyond the aforesaid bounds as
they shall have occasion, the lands lying within being in-
tended for plowing, home pastures and meadow lands only."[2]
The lease to Codrington curtailed this liberty, but the New
York claim was that such commonage was not a sufficient
appropriation to take any land west of the Harlem line out of
the Dongan Charter, and also that the Dongan patent of
March, 1686, confirming the Nichols patent[3] expressly cuts
off this outside commonage.   In spite of repeated opposition
on the part of the Harlem freeholders, this claim was made
good till just prior to the revolution.   The Codrington lease
and subsequent leases of outlying land generally, previous to
1760, seem to have been made rather to protect the commons
from encroachment than for revenue.   The rent reserved on
the sixty acres was sixpence per acre.

From 1704 to 1732 there was little change relative
to the subject in hand.   The income and expenditures of the
corporation show a monotonous moderation and a good balance on the right side.   For ten years ending 1730, the
average annual expenditure was three hundred and thirty-five

[1] Map II.
[2] Riker's *History of Harlem*, p. 252.
[3] *Ibid*, 465.

pounds,[1] and the average surplus over one hundred pounds. No local taxation other than the poor rate was necessary, except in 1717, when the legislature authorized a levy of five hundred pounds for altering the course of the common sewer at the end of Broad street, and for cleansing and scouring the dock. The ferry, the chief source of revenue, was made more productive by securing under the Cornbury charter of 1708, the land between high and low water mark on the Long Island side from Wall about to Red Hook, a measure by which the competition of individuals was curtailed. The ferry was rented in 1710 for one hundred and eighty pounds, and the dock for thirty pounds.

In 1719, with an expenditure of two hundred and fifty-two pounds, a surplus remained of two hundred and forty-three pounds. This was partly due to the sale of two hundred and thirty front feet of water lots between Beekman and Peck slips to the holders of the adjacent upland at their request. The price was one hundred and twelve pounds. Some of the purchasers of former grants now sought of the governor and council the privilege of gaining ground out of the river in their front. The corporation protested and began to press for a grant to itself "of all that may be gained out of the rivers around the island." Efforts to secure this and further concessions were incited by the wiping out of the surplus under expenses of 1723 and 1724, occasioned by "the ruinous condition of the great dock and of all its walls through the storm of July last." Finally in 1730 the Montgomery charter was secured. It gave the city complete and exclusive right of ferri-

---

[1] This expenditure seems remarkably small for a town of from six to eight thousand people. Under the law of 1691, however, much could be assessed back on the property benefited. The mayor and aldermen received no salary, though the mayor had the market fees. The treasurer received a commission. The poor were under the care of the church wardens. The only salaries in 1710 were for the town clerk, marshal and bellmen or watch, which amounted to £66. The remaining expenditure, £191, was chiefly for repairs to corporation property, and £42 sundries.

age and marketage, and four hundred feet beyond low water mark from Charlton street to the fort and from White Hall to Colear's Hook.

The deliberations over this charter were protracted, and the expense to the city of preparing and supporting it considerable. One thousand pounds for the purpose were secured on a mortgage of the most valuable lots the city possessed, those seven making two small blocks[1] between Moore street and Whitehall, Pearl, Water and Front, where a portion of the old dock had been. To discharge the mortgage it was thought best to sell the lots, and in 1732 they were purchased at auction by the principal merchants of the city for one thousand three hundred and forty-four pounds. This sale was the last of any account under the policy of disposing of the water lots in fee. By it the city parted with the last of its ground between the original high and low water lines, from Whitehall to James street or about the end of Cherry street, as shown on Lyne's map, save the lot at Peck slip.[2] Beginning with 1734, the policy was adopted of reserving an annual rent upon the water lots granted, and their history branches off from that of the upland. In granting them a few spaces were reserved, which the corporation afterward filled up and sold, as will be noticed hereinafter.

Lyne's map shows that the city was now extending into the vicinity of the lower commons. Beekman's swamp lay in the way, the lease of it had expired, and the city had already in 1728 sold ten lots of it to Jacobus Roosevelt for one hundred pounds, the money being appropriated "to the use of building a new powder house and to no other purpose whatsoever." The site selected for the powder house is interesting, as it afterwards became valuable for city lots. It is shown on Lyne's map, and was "a small island near the land to the

---

[1] Map I. Blocks W and X. The frontage of each block on Water street is 100 feet; the depth 108 and 136 respectively. The distances are from the deeds.

[2] Map I.

southward of fresh water." In 1734 the whole tract of Beekman's swamp, four and a half acres,[1] was sold to Mr. Roosevelt for one hundred pounds in addition to the one hundred
pounds already paid for the ten lots. It still goes by the
name of the swamp, and has continued to be the seat of the
leather trade since tan-pits were dug there early in the last
century.

[1] Map I.

2. 1734-1755

FIXED ANNUAL QUIT-RENTS RESERVED IN GRANTING WATER LOTS.

UPLAND LEASED

The revenues or the city were now again ample for its expenditure, without recourse to other taxation than the poor rate, or to borrowing, or to sales of land; and so continued till 1750, except for a tax of two hundred and fifty pounds in 1737 for repairs to the city hall, and another of five hundred and seventy-four pounds in 1741 for increasing the night watch after the negro riots. In 1741, also, a small amount yearly was tacked on the minister's and poor's rate to keep in repair the wells and pumps. By act of 1753 it was not to exceed one hundred and twenty pounds. Meanwhile watch-houses and the first almshouse were built; and the latter, on the site of the present city hall, marked a yearly increasing expense for the poor coincident with the war of 1744-48. In 1747 this amounted to seven hundred pounds, or as much as the city revenue from its property, licenses and freedoms.

The population increased slowly from eight thousand six hundred and twenty-two slave and free in 1731, to thirteen thousand and forty white and black in 1756, of whom two thousand three hundred and sixty-eight were black and for the most part slaves. During the thirty-five years preceding 1731, the population had just about doubled.[1]

The grant of an isolated tract of ten acres of swamp land fronting on the present Broadway at Eighteenth, Nineteenth and Twentieth streets[2] was made by exception during this period to Admiral Peter Warren in 1744 at four pounds annual rent forever, "in consideration of his distinguished services in behalf of the kingdom and the city." In 1750-51 the

---

[1] The figures are taken from O'Callaghan's *Documentary History of New York.*

[2] The tract is shown on Holmes' map of Sir Peter Warren's estate. It extends six hundred feet west from Broadway.

cost of building a corporation pier at Coenties slip was paid with money borrowed on the credit of the corporation to the extent of eight hundred and sixty pounds.   This proved to be the beginning of a system of borrowing which in twenty-five years saddled the city with a debt of thirteen thousand pounds at five and six per cent.   And this notwithstanding the growth of the annual water rents from two hundred and thirty pounds in 1761 to eight hundred and thirty pounds in 1775; an average annual city rate after 1758 of sixteen hundred pounds, applied for specifically each year and tacked on the minister's and poor's rate;[1] and lotteries by which one thousand pounds was raised in each of the years 1756, 1757 and 1758, and three thousand pounds more towards enlarging the city hall in 1762.   The important permanent acquisitions were a new gaol in 1756 and 1757; Bedloe's Island purchased for a pest-house in 1758, for one thousand pounds; barracks on the common for eight hundred men in 1758, three thousand and five hundred pounds; five hundred stand of arms, 1758; public lamps first placed in 1761; extension of the city hall,

---

[1] By a law of 1764 the amount that might be tacked to this rate for wells and pumps was increased to two hundred pounds.   The same year the amount annually required for the maintainence of roads and highways outside the city proper was tacked on also; in 1769 it was two hundred and sixty-eight pounds, and the cost of the poor about three thousand pounds, four times the cost in 1747.   An act of 1761 authorized a tax of one thousand eight hundred pounds for fixing of lamps and providing a sufficient number of watchmen, and thereafter it was for watch and lamps that the one thousand six hundred pounds was required.   The separation of church and state at the revolution left the vestry without authority to levy any tax, and conferred no equivalent authority on the corporation, which henceforth made annual application to the assembly to levy a definite sum for its public charge, including the cost of the poor.   This was voted in two items, the one chargeable on both city wards and the out ward; the other only on that more thickly settled part of the island south of a line indicated in the tax law for the year, or therein left to be fixed by a city ordinance.   The latter was the city rate, the former the city and county rate.   It was in effect only the city rate that before the revolution had to be applied for every time it was levied.   The watch rate was extended to city and county in 1846, but street cleaning and lamp rates continued to be levied south of the line only until 1863.

1762, seven thousand pounds; a square of two hundred and forty-eight feet on Broadway in the midst of the commons, hitherto owned by private individuals, in 1760, one thousand seven hundred and thirteen pounds; the Bridewell or city prison 1768-1769, not finally completed till after the revolution.[1]

During all this period the policy of holding on to the common lands was continued, in spite of the increase of debt and the burden of taxation. An attempt was also made to get a better revenue from them by cutting up portions of them into building lots. One portion was the old common pasture of New Amsterdam. The Boston post road, later Chatham street and now Park Row, divided it in two sections, with a third adjacent triangular block now covered by the Times and Potter buildings.[2] The eastern section is shown on Lyne's map as a triangular tract bounded by the post road, the road which continues Queen street, and a connecting road. In 1759 a portion of the west section was surveyed into fifty-nine lots, as shown on map III.[3] The northern boundary of the corporation land here was at the time in dispute. It was partially adjusted by an exchange deed in 1768,[4] but not finally until 1800, when the corporation received the ground within and to the south of Chambers street to Broadway, and released its remaining lots to the north as far east as Augustus street, besides lots 26, 27 and 28 east of Augustus street, to even up the exchange. Meanwhile the lots as first surveyed were offered to lease for between two and four pounds annually.

With the close of the war in 1760 the city began to grow

[1] The gaol, barracks and Bridewell were built on the common near the Almshouse, as shown in Maps III and VIII.

[2] Map I.

[3] The location of these lots in relation to present streets will appear on comparing Maps III and VIII.

[4] Map III.

rapidly, and by 1771 had reached a population of twenty-two thousand. Private enterprise opened up new sections to the northwest and northeast of the commons, and speculative values developed. In 1762 the commons east of the post road were laid out into lots,[1] and the city surveyor was instructed to offer them for twenty-one years at four pounds each per annum. The following year one hundred and fifty acres of the upper commons were staked off into lots of approximately five acres each, known as the Inclenberg lots, and most of them leased at auction. They were bid off for more than some of the purchasers were afterwards willing to pay, and after several concessions, a final deduction was made in 1772 of one-half the rent from the time of leasing, and the term made thirty-five years " from May 1st next." The lessees set forth that they had cultivated their lands, but as the land was poor soil they could not make the yearly rent out of them. Ten acres of this land was leased for thirty-three years in 1773, presumably at the reduced rates, for sixteen shillings per acre annually.

From this uniform policy of leasing for a term of years there were but two or three departures of any account until after the revolution. One of these was a perpetual lease to the Reformed Protestant Dutch Church for a burial ground in 1766, of a block of twenty-eight lots bounded by Thomas, Queen and King George streets, now Duane and Rose, Pearl and William.[2] The rent reserved was seventy pounds annually, about what the lots were worth at the time; and there was a condition not to " convert the same at any time for ever hereafter to private uses." It was released in 1790, when the corporation was hard pressed for money, in consideration of one thousand pounds. A similar grant was made the same year to the English Presbyterian Church, which in its petition cited " the distinguished generosity by which our brethren of

[1] Map IV, and compare Map XIV.

[2] Map IV.

Trinity Church were supplied with a large and convenient burying ground of the free gift of this honorable board." This church particularly desired the triangle between Beekman street, the post road and Nassau street, already mentioned as to-day occupied by the Times and Potter buildings. After some negotiation in which they were offered the block west of the Dutch church, but thought it too remote, their petition was granted and a perpetual lease ordered at forty pounds a year, eighteen pounds and fifteen shillings of which was released on petition in 1784 the old rent being then thought "too high for the quantity of land contained." As usual, there was the condition that it should not be applied to private secular uses, a reservation that turned out to be of considerable value to the city; for in 1856, on an agreement to release the condition for one-fourth the proceeds of the sale of the ground at public auction at a minimum price of two hundred and twenty-five thousand dollars, the city received as its share sixty-seven thousand five hundred dollars.

The revolution was now at hand. In the closing days of peace the award of the commissioners appointed under the act of 1772 to settle the interminable dispute over the Harlem commons was confirmed.[1] It was adverse to New York, and gave the Harlem freeholders in lieu of their indefinite commonage a triangular tract of two hundred and ninety acres; west of the Harlem line.[2] The acquisition proved of little use to Harlem. It lay remote and unimproved, and once out of the city's hands, liable to taxation and assessments. Accumulation of these, especially on the opening of Third avenue, foreshadowed a forced sale of the property, to avoid which an act of the legislature was obtained in 1820 vesting the land in trustees for making sales, and applying the proceeds after paying taxes and assessments to the benefit of the town library and certain schools. The trustees, after having once in 1823

[1] Law of April 3d, 1775.
[2] Map II.

offered to sell the whole tract to the city, in 1825 sold almost all the two hundred and ninety acres, over five thousand city lots, for twenty-five thousand five hundred dollars, to Dudley Selden, from whom present titles are traced.[1]

During the revolution the city remained in the hands of the British troops, and there was no regular municipal organization. The old vestry, however, seems to have performed some public functions, and certainly received corporation rents.

---

[1] For a very complete account of the controversy over the Harlem Commons, showing the title into Dudley Selden, and his conveyances down to 1838, see pamphlet prepared by Isaac Adriance.

3.   1784–1802

POLICY OF LEASING BUILDING LOTS CONTINUED, BUT ONE-HALF
OF UPPER COMMONS SOLD IN FEE

In February 1784, the meetings of the common council were resumed.   During the war five thousand five hundred pounds unpaid interest on the city debt had accumulated, the public buildings required overhauling, and the Bridewell was still to be finished.   There had been, of course, accumulation of unpaid rents, but most of the leases except at Inclenberg had expired, and there was difficulty in adjusting arrears.   As a special committee to look into the matter sets forth: "Arrears of rent are due to the corporation from many meritorious persons who have taken an active and decided part in the cause of their country, and suffered all the inconveniences of exile and the loss of all their possessions.   Many other persons well affected to the cause of their country, lessees to this corporation, who left the city in the year 1776, have from poverty and other unavoidable causes been obliged to return within the British lines before the peace took place, and have been prevented from occupying their habitations and deriving any advantage from their leased estates because of their attachment to the American cause, but upon condition of their paying rent to the vestry or Mr. Smyth their treasurer." "In the first case it will, in the opinion of the committee, be inconsistent with the rules of equity to expect from such well attached returning exiles the rents which became in arrears from the time of their leaving the city in 1776 to the time of their occupying their respective estates on the 25th of November last." "In the second case, the committee are of the opinion that no rent ought in justice to be exacted from the citizens who were and continue well attached to the American cause, and actually paid rent to Mr. Smyth for the period of time they actually paid rent as aforesaid."

The report was approved, and it was further ordered " that no allowance or abatement to any person or persons whomsoever who are grantees of the corporation be made for any rents which became due prior to the first day of May, 1776, or subsequent to the 25 November last." This arrangement was not satisfactory to a number of tenants, but was nevertheless enforced when necessary by sale of the lessees' improvements. It was amended the next year by a resolution that all dues to the corporation for real estate accruing between May, 1776, and November 24th, 1783, be remitted, provided that the debtors shall swear or prove by some other person that " he or she or they have resided out of the British lines during the late war, and have not directly or indirectly received any rent or other emolument whatever," from the property during that time. On this basis there were collected up to September, 1785, seven thousand four hundred pounds, including accruing rent on the new leases, which were generally for twenty-one years, and at about fifty per cent. advance over rates before the war, six pounds being the usual yearly rent for lots east of Chatham street. Besides enforcing to this extent the collection of rents, a ten thousand pound tax was raised as against six thousand six hundred and thirty-one the last year before the war, four thousand two hundred and thirty-three of which had been " for the cost of the poor." After an unsuccessful attempt to secure a part of the proceeds of confiscated estates in the city, the corporation, in 1785, sold twelve lots gained from the water, three made out of the corporation lot on the west corner of Water street and Peck slip, on which there stood one brick building of twenty-five feet front, for two thousand three hundred and eighty pounds, and nine near the corporation wharf at the North river for three thousand one hundred and seventy pounds.[1] These sales,

[1] The block of which the nine lots are the western portion is that bounded by Fulton, Vesey, Greenwich and Washington Streets. It had been reserved for a market site in granting the water lots, and there was a market house on part of the eastern portion and fronting Greenwich St.

however, only met the emergencies of the moment, leaving the old debt of thirteen thousand pounds and four thousand two hundred pounds interest still unpaid. To pay this off it was proposed to sell outright a portion of the commons, and with some circumspection in breaking a precedent that had kept the commons intact for more than a century the plan was proceeded with.

In May 1785, a survey had been ordered " of the vacant land belonging to the corporation situated between the post and Bloomingdale roads, into lots as near as may be of five acres each and numbered, leaving a middle road between the two said roads."[1] The following December the city surveyor presented his map, and a committee was appointed to see how the lots could best be disposed of. In February the committee advised a sale in fee of part of the lots if a reasonable price could be obtained. It was not, however, till the spring of 1789, when the times were more propitious, that a sale was ordered. The purchasers were to pay one-tenth within ten days after the sale, and to have five years for the payment of the residue, with interest at five per cent., the debts or bonds against the corporation to be discounted in payment. On these terms one hundred and ninety acres were sold to seven purchasers, partly at auction, and partly at private sale to some who held leases.[2] The receipts for the one hundred and ninety acres were five thousand four hundred pounds, an average of about twenty-eight pounds, or seventy dollars, an acre. One hundred and five acres of the land sold lay within that portion of the commons bounded very closely by the present Thirty-second and Forty-second streets, Broadway and Lexington avenue, leaving there thirty acres still the property of the city though under lease, with fifteen acres more known as the powder house lots and adjacent on the

[1] These lots are a portion of those shown on Map V.

[2] The specific tract sold each individual and the price are shown on Map V below Forty-eighth street, which is marked at its intersection with the middle road.

south, held unoccupied in reserve.[1] Of the remaining eighty-five acres sold, ten lay adjacent to the powder house lots on the south, and seventy-five between Forty-second and Forty-eighth streets, Third and Fifth avenues.[2] Westward of this portion the commons, as surveyed by Goerck in 1796, extended nearly to the present Sixth avenue, widening out to near Seventh avenue at Sixty-fourth street and to Second avenue at Sixty-seventh street, and then continuing within or near the lines of these avenues until they are cut by the line of the Harlem commons at Ninety-third street and Seventy-ninth street respectively. The whole commons as thus constituted contained about eleven hundred acres.[3]

Hardly more than an eighth of what remained after the sale of 1789 could be divided into five-acre lots so as to front on some then existing road. The rest was hemmed in by the land of private owners, and being for the most part rough and rocky, had little value until future streets should be at least in sight. This may in part explain an apparently ill-considered private sale of fifty acres in 1792, for less than thirty dollars an acre. It lay immediately in the rear of the premises of the purchasers, and within the lines of Fifty-seventh and Sixty-fifth streets, and Third and Fourth avenues.[3]

Between 1790 and 1800, the city's growth was phenomenal. The population doubled to sixty thousand, the assessed valuation nearly quadrupled to twenty millions. It was clear that the city was destined to future greatness, and forecasts began to be made as to stages in the advance. A far-sighted policy could hardly fail to suggest itself as to the commons. In February 1796, the committee on common lands reported

[1] Map VII, which shows the original lots with the present streets cut through them. The leased lots are numbered 16, 17, 18, 21 and 22. The powder house lots 31, 32 and 33.

[2] Map V.

[3] Maps V and VI. The key to locations on these maps above Forty-second street, is found in the figures and lines on the Middle Road, which shows the intersection of present streets and Fifth avenue.

"that they have had a survey made of the commons, contemplating that the same may hereafter be improved as part of the city, to which end they have streets regularly laid down. They are unanimously of opinion that the best mode of improving the same, is to sell at public vendue the one-half, and to lease the other for a term of years. They are induced to recommend this plan from a belief that it will tend to a speedy improvement, and that the one-half which is to be leased will at the end of the term be worth more than the whole now is."

The sale as recommended took place in June, with the same conditions as to the time of payment as in 1789. Fifty-eight alternate lots were disposed of to forty-one purchasers, for an aggregate of seventeen thousand six hundred pounds, or about sixty-six pounds or one hundred and sixty-five dollars an acre for two hundred and sixty-six acres. There was also a quit-rent reserved of four bushels of wheat per lot, and each purchaser had the option, quite generally taken, to lease an adjacent lot for twenty-one years at four pounds per year. The buying was speculative as compared with the rates of 1789, which were based on farm values. Many of the purchasers seem to have regretted their bargains, and failed to claim no less than twenty-six of the fifty-eight lots sold. Twenty-one of these were resold in 1801 at a reduction of forty per cent from the prices of 1796.[1] The lots lying east of Third avenue and north of Sixty-sixth street were held back at the request of adjacent owners who desired them at private sale, as the lots if sold to others would cut them off from the post road. The board valued these lots at from one hundred and sixty pounds to two hundred pounds, and a quit rent of one bushel of wheat per acre. Thirty-three and a quarter acres were taken at the former price by one owner, three and two-sevenths acres at the latter price by another,

[1] Maps V and VI. The prices obtained in 1796 are marked on each lot in pounds; those obtained in 1801, in dollars. Lots sold later are dated. In two or three cases the same price is marked twice on a lot, as a means of showing more clearly its extent.

and lots 202 and 204 were sold to a third purchaser at one hundred and sixty pounds per acre for twelve hundred and thirty pounds.[1] These sales made the aggregate area so far disposed of in the upper commons just about one-half the whole.

By help of receipts from sales of 1789 and 1796, the city was able to close the century with a debt but very little larger than it was in 1775, namely, thirteen thousand five hundred pounds as against twelve thousand eight hundred pounds. During the decade it had moreover built a new almshouse on the common in the rear of the old one,[2] defraying the greater part of the cost, however, from ten thousand pounds proceeds of a lottery granted by the state; leveled the fort under the act of 1790, though the state still held the site; improved that portion of the present Battery granted by the act aforesaid; purchased land at Bellevue for three thousand eight hundred pounds, and erected a hospital building there for the state health office, which was however disused on the opening, soon after, of a state establishment on Bedloe's Island; and acquired also ninety lots for a Potter's field, being the greater part of the present Washington Square, at a cost of one thousand eight hundred pounds.

[1] Map VI.
[2] Map VIII.

4.   1803–1815

EXTENSIVE PERMANENT IMPROVEMENTS PAID FOR BY SALE OF NEW BUILDING-LOTS.   UPPER COMMONS AND MOST OF OLD BUILDING-LOTS LEASED

In pursuance of the policy adopted in 1796, the unsold half of the upper commons was held in reserve.   In one or two cases a purchaser was allowed to exchange his lot for another. In one case, in 1810, assurance that the lessee of one of the alternate lots should have a renewal at the expiration of his lease was refused, on the ground that the alternate lots were " leased with the expectation and on the plan that by their increase in value through the improvements on the lots sold in fee, the corporation should reap substantial advantage, and that to extend the lease and in any way bind the corporation so that it could not take advantage of this increase at the end of the lease would be to abandon the original plan and establish a precedent that might seriously interfere with the possible revenue of the corporation."

In 1805 the leases of lots on the lower commons began to fall in.[1]   The old leases had been for twenty-one years at from ten to fifteen dollars rent.   Where they had not been improved and the lease expired, the new lease was sold at auction, with the condition that a brick building of at least two stories and a garret should be built, which improvements should be valued at the end of the term by appraisers reciprocally chosen and a new rent, fixed by the corporation, agreed to, or the buildings surrendered at the valuation.   With those who had improved their lots private agreements were made on the same

[1] Jan. 1803, the corporation had eighty-four lots on lease beside the alternate lots of common lands:—seventy-one on the lower commons; seven along the west side of Peck slip to Front street, filled out in front of the lots sold in 1785; six at Inclenberg, being part of the five acre lots reserved below Forty-second street in the upper commons.   Of these leases three expired in 1804, thirteen in 1805, thirty in 1806, twelve in 1807 and 1808, and the rest between 1813 and 1826.

basis.   But in some cases these lots too were offered at auction,
the corporation taking the buildings at its own appraisal.
Lots thirty feet wide on the south side of Chatham street were
re-rented for two hundred and fifty dollars; twenty-five feet lots
on the north side for two hundred dollars.   Lots on Thomas,
Augustus and William streets brought ninety and one hundred dollars ; small lots less than twenty-five feet square at Peck
slip, one hundred and twenty-five dollars.   There was at this
time, as these increased rents indicate, a prevalent confidence
in the future rapid growth of the city.   The census of 1805
showed an increase of population of twenty-five per cent. in
five years.   It was predicted that the city would contain seven
hundred thousand inhabitants in 1855, and over three million
in 1890.[1]

The conditions favoring, the city laid out fifty-nine half-
acre lots at Inclenberg—where there were thirty acres[2] the
leases of which had just expired—with the intention of offering them to lease; but the city was now borrowing at the rate
of forty thousand dollars a year for the new city hall alone,
and the opening of Canal street was in hand.   A com-
promise between selling and leasing was effected by offering the lots at auction on perpetual lease, with a reservation of
twenty bushels of wheat or its equivalent in money on each lot
per annum.   The fifty-nine lots, sold on these terms to about
half that number of purchasers, brought sixty-two thousand
dollars, or at the rate of about two thousand dollars an acre .
for lands surrounded by those which in 1789 had been sold at
seventy dollars.   It was more than the lots turned out to
be worth and a few years later, when under the act of 1807 the
new streets were laid down in such a way as would spoil their
lots, the purchasers generally accepted the city's offer to
take back the lots and repay the money with interest, in bonds
running two, three and four years from 1811.   A similar dis-

[1] *Daily Advertiser*, April, 1806.

[2] Map V, Lots 16, 17, 18, 21, 22, 25, 26.

position was made of the Dove lots, so called, a square of about twenty acres, bounded nearly by Fourth and Third avenues, Sixty-fifth and Sixty-ninth streets,[1] and which, as under lease, had not been sold in 1796. This tract was plotted out by the city, so that a public parkway two hundred and fifty feet wide should run through its centre and be intersected by a street between the avenues. A square of one hundred and twenty-five feet was reserved for a church and academy. The twenty-eight lots left, most of them sixty-two by three hundred and sixty-five feet, were sold at auction in the spring of 1807 for a total of twenty-one thousand dollars and a quit-rent of twenty bushels of wheat per lot.

By this time a third public work of considerable magnitude was under way, namely the filling up of the fresh water or Collect, as it was now called, a deep pond just north of the lower commons. It was connected with either river by swamp land, through which its outlet ran eastward, crossing Pearl street, as may be seen in Lyne's map.[2] The extensive marsh on the west along the line of Canal street had been expressly reserved from the Dongan Charter, and in 1733 was granted to Anthony Rutgers by George II., saving the rights of the city to the pond and the island, on which stood the powder house. To secure its title to the pond beyond doubt, the city purchased of Rutgers' heirs, in 1791, all their claim or right to the soil under water, paying therefor one hundred and fifty pounds. The following year a strip of the land between the Collect and Broadway was purchased of the executors of Mary Barclay for three hundred and fifty pounds, making the original cost to the city of its Collect property five hundred pounds. A canal connecting the two rivers had been proposed, on the supposition that there might be sufficient difference of tidal level, which subsequent measurements did not confirm. Finally it was determined to drain the swamp

[1] Map VI.
[2] Map I.

by a channel in Canal street, and to fill up the Collect. As soon as the strip of swamp towards Broadway was reclaimed, its site value and the same causes that induced the sales of 1806 and 1807 led to the offering of the new lots at auction. Twenty lots sold to seven different purchasers in 1809 brought twenty-five thousand five hundred and twenty dollars.[1]

The old powder magazine was now out of place in the neighborhood of the Collect, but as the common council had assented to the keeping the state powder there, the legislature was petitioned to provide another building within the city. Under the act of 1808, supplemented by that of 1809, the governor purchased two of the five-acre common land lots, numbers 102 and 103, as a site for a new state magazine.[2] One of the lots was under lease from the city, the other was private property subject to a quit-rent to the city of four bushels of wheat annually. For its interest in the two lots the corporation received seven hundred dollars. The old powder house site was cut up into seven lots, five of which, with the three lots west of Elm street,[3] were leased in 1811 for twenty-one years at from seventy-five to one hundred and thirty-five dollars each. At the same time six lots at Peck slip, where the city had lately filled in from Front to South street a strip fifty feet wide in front of its other lots, were leased at auction for twenty-one years, the corner lot at South street, seventeen feet by fifty, for five hundred and eighty dollars, the others at from two hundred and ninety to four hundred and fifteen dollars. The lessees, however, found the filling in defective, and after a deduction of one-half the rent had been offered them, the lots were sold in fee for twenty-one thousand four hundred and fifty dollars, about four dollars per square foot.

[1] They are those marked alphabetically on Map VIII. Lot B was bid in by the city for three thousand eight hundred dollars, and shortly after sold at private sale for four thousand dollars.

[2] Map VI.

[3] Map VIII.

By the beginning of the year 1812 the city debt had become a matter of serious concern. Since 1803 the cost of the city hall, four hundred and twenty-five thousand dollars; advances for property taken for Canal street, one hundred thousand dollars; land at the foot of Dey street, where the corporation proposed to fill in and sell lots, sixty-five thousand dollars; six and one-fourth acres more at Bellevue, to receive the almshouse when removed, twenty-two thousand five hundred dollars; and the first year's expenditure on the new almshouse and penitentiary there, seventy-five thousand dollars—in all nearly seven hundred thousand dollars, had been met with bonds or money borrowed on the bonds of the city at six and seven per cent. These bonds were very numerous, constantly falling due, and a source of annoyance and embarrassment. In view of these conditions the common council, by a vote of ten to three, resolved to petition the legislature for leave to create a six per cent. public stock of nine hundred thousand dollars with which to fund this debt and to finish the city hall and Bellevue buildings. The cost of taking public squares laid out under the act of 1807 was also pleaded, but in fact was not incurred for some years. The act authorizing the issue was passed in June, 1812.

Meanwhile a sale of the newly filled Collect lots was ordered, and thirty-four of them were disposed of at auction in April, 1812 to eighteen purchasers for twenty-two thousand dollars.[1] The corner lot at the old city hall, head of Broad street, twenty-five by one hundred and twelve feet, was also sold for nine thousand five hundred dollars. In June, on the recommendation of the market committee, it was voted to sell seven lots near the Hudson market on Greenwich street, being the rest of the block part of which had been sold in 1785, and to set aside the proceeds to build Washington market on the block newly filled in front.

The report of the comptroller in January, 1813, showing an

[1] Map VIII.

expenditure on the Bellevue buildings for the year of eighty-one thousand dollars, and of ninety thousand dollars towards the completion of the city hall, was followed by a vote to sell three lots at the old city hall, and five others of which the city had bought in the lease prior to extending Chambers street to Chatham.

The three remaining city hall lots, twenty-three, twenty-six and one-half and twenty-seven feet by one hundred and twelve feet, produced twenty-five thousand dollars; the five Chambers street lots,[1] thirteen thousand eight hundred dollars; and the seven Greenwich street lots, thirty-four thousand and fifty dollars; making the total sales within a year's time over one hundred thousand dollars. Of the stock, six hundred thousand dollars had been at once sold July 9th, 1812, and one hundred thousand dollars more in December.

In the spring of 1813 a suit to decide whether the lessees should pay any of the assessment for opening Chambers street to Chatham was decided in favor of the corporation. As a portion of some of the lots benefited had been taken for the new street, damages had also to be awarded some tenants. To determine whether the jury had awarded these fairly, a committee of the common council laid down the correct but very abstractly stated principle, "that the damages allowed ought to be such as after deducting the assessment would leave a principal the interest of which, added to an apportionment of the principal itself among the years yet to come of the term demised, would so reduce the original rent as to leave a just reservation on those portions of the lots which still remain."

The year 1813 was further marked by the establishment of the sinking fund, with which the after-history of the city property in land is so closely connected that a restatement of the views of its founders seems warranted. The comptroller in a report of the 19th of April had pointed out that

[1] Map XIV. Lots 17 and i-iv inclusive.

the total amount of the debt or stock outstanding, seven
hundred thousand dollars, did not exceed the cost of the City
Hall and Bellevue buildings,[1] and this he regarded as a proof
that the city's ordinary receipts from taxes and revenue would
be sufficient for its ordinary expenses. The one hundred
thousand dollars lately obtained from sales of public lands he
balanced with the further extraordinary outlay for the Varick
basin, the opening of Chambers street and other minor improvements. He argued that with the completion of the Bellevue
establishment the extraordinary expenditures would cease for
some time to come, and that so far as there should be a normal increase in the city's expenses, the normal increase in the
city revenue might be expected to meet it; that therefore
the city debt could be wiped out by the establishment of a
sinking fund, which he proposed should be administered by
the mayor, the chairman of the finance committee, the cham-
berlain and the comptroller. To this fund he would appropriate:

1. Commutation of quit-rents on water grants prior to 1804.
2. Mayoralty fees.
3. Market fees.
4. Cab, vault and pawnbrokers' licenses.
5. Twenty-five per cent. of all proceeds of city property sold
in fee.

He estimated that the accumulation of quit-rents up to December 31st, 1826, when the stock fell due, would yield a
principal and interest of seventy-five thousand dollars; that
market and mayor's fees and licenses would yield nine thous-
and dollars a year, which, with the interest applied quarterly,

---

[1] The cost of the present city hall up to 1813 was five hundred and twelve
thousand dollars. It was finished in 1814 after a further expenditure of twenty-
six thousand dollars.

The Bellevue buildings, almshouse, penitentiary, and workshops, begun in
1812, had cost up to 1813 one hundred and twenty-six thousand dollars. They
were finished in 1817, at a total cost of four hundred and twenty-one thousand
dollars.

would produce one hundred and eighty thousand dollars; and that twenty-five per cent. of sales of public property up to 1827, with interest, would swell the total to four hundred thousand dollars, leaving of the seven hundred thousand dollars city debt then existing three hundred thousand dollars still unprovided for. To meet this there were eighty five-acre lots of common lands the leases of which would expire in 1824, and which then might be sold to extinguish the rest of the debt, or the balance of the stock might be extended ten or twelve years, by which time the sinking fund would extinguish it. In July the finance committee reported favorably upon the plan, with the amendment that the proceeds of the sale of the government house lots presently to be mentioned should go entirely to the fund. Until a special law establishing the board could be secured, a sinking fund committee as recommended by the comptroller, with the addition of the recorder, was appointed to carry out the plan.

The government house property, so called, was a part of the fort which, as excepted from the Dongan Charter and held by crown, passed to the state at the revolution. Under the law of 1812, amended by that of 1813, the corporation purchased of the state unconditionally the government house which had been erected on the site of the fort and facing Bowling Green, together with the grounds immediately in the rear. Shortly afterward the state ceded the rest of the block to the United States for defence purposes, but through the exertions of the city comptroller, Thomas Mercein, who proposed and conducted the negotiations, conveyance was made to the city by the state and United States, in return for ground at the Narrows purchased by the city and transferred to the United States.[1] The corporation now having possession of the whole square bounded by the Bowling Green, Whitehall, Bridge and State streets, laid it out in seventeen lots,[2] which were sold at auc-

---

[1] The state's share in this transaction was authorized by chap. xiii., amended by chap. xxviii., laws of 1814.

[2] Map IX.

tion in the spring of 1815 on terms very advantageous to the city. The comptroller's account epitomizes the result as follows:

ACCOUNT GOVERNMENT HOUSE GROUNDS NEGOTIATIONS.

To cash paid state	$50,000	By cash received for lots	$158,200
Narrows for U. S.	19,335	Buildings	6,287
Int. on first purchase	2,000	Rent	1,463
For the buildings	14,245		
Net Gain	80,370		
	$165,950		$165,950

The proceeds were not, however, paid into the sinking fund but used directly, eighty per cent. gross of them to take up still outstanding city bonds, which were thereby all cancelled except one of eighteen thousand five hundred dollars. The debt of the city was thus reduced to the seven hundred thousand dollars outstanding stock. The sinking fund received an addition, however, shortly after, of the commutations of wheat quit-rents on common lands. This was voted in February, 1816, on the report of the comptroller in which he argued that "to allow commutation would conduce to improvements on the sold lots, and so benefit the alternate leased lots, and that as the common land embraces a property which it is presumed will hereafter add much to the resources of the corporation, every encouragement ought to be given to render it more valuable." The quit-rents were accordingly allowed to be commuted at six per cent., reckoning wheat at two dollars the bushel. This was in March, 1816. In February, 1817, the White street quit-rents[1] were allowed to be commuted, but at two dollars and a half the bushel.

[1] Map VIII, lettered lots.

5. 1816–1821

REPETITION OF FORMER EXPERIENCE OF SALES AFTER WAR AS
TO DOWNTOWN LOTS, BUT RESIDUE OF UPPER COMMONS
STILL UNDER LEASE

Between May, 1816, and May, 1820, the ordinary receipts
fell behind the ordinary expenditures two hundred and ten
thousand dollars, while the extra payments amounted to
three hundred and ninety thousand dollars. Neither were
any large enterprises on hand during the period, like the City
Hall and Bellevue establishment, except that forty-three thousand dollars of the cost of the latter fell in the years 1816 and
1817. Forty-seven thousand dollars were spent in filling the
Varick basin and making its bulkheads; twenty-seven thousand dollars in paying the bonds given Mr. Varick; and twelve
thousand dollars in filling another block between King and
Charlton streets that had been reserved in granting water lots.
The total of other valuable acquisitions and improvements, ex-
cepting Oliver street, eighteen thousand dollars; Canal street
final awards, seventeen thousand dollars, and the ninth ward
avenues and streets, seventy-six thousand dollars, some of
which would come back in assessments, did not much exceed
one hundred thousand dollars for the four years.[1] The
deficit must be ascribed to the industrial depression that followed the war, and culminated in the crisis of 1819, and to
unwillingness under the circumstances to close the era of low
taxation that had hitherto prevailed, as shown by the low val-
uations of the years previous to 1815 and then by the low rates,
less than four dollars and a half on one thousand up to 1820.
During the war, also, bills of credit had been issued by the corporation, and one hundred and thirty-five thousand dollars of

[1] These data are taken from the comptroller's report entered on the common
council minutes of April 20, 1820, in which he reviews the fiscal transactions of
the four years preceding.

these had to be redeemed between 1816 and 1820. To meet
the deficit temporary loans were obtained, amounting to two
hundred and twenty-five thousand dollars; the reserve of
the nine hundred thousand dollars stock of 1812 was sold,
one hundred thousand in June, 1817, and one hundred thous-
and in September, 1819; and for the rest, sales of land
were made between the two issues of stock as follows:
twenty-nine more Collect lots were sold at auction in Feb.
1818 for twenty-five thousand three hundred and twenty-
five dollars, twenty-two of them to a single purchaser,[1] thirty-
five out of forty-five acres of land at Bloomingdale[2] which had
been turned over to the corporation by an official to square
his accounts were sold at the same time for twelve thousand
one hundred and seventy dollars; also the remaining curtailed
lots in the angle north of Chambers street and east of Augustus, for seven thousand one hundred eighty-five dollars;[3] fourteen lots at the Albany basin sold in October, 1818, brought
forty-seven thousand eight hundred dollars;[4] and twenty-two
lots at the Varick basin, similarly sold in January, 1816,
brought one hundred and twenty-seven thousand dollars.[5]
The Albany basin lots were the first and the southernmost of the
blocks reserved in granting the water lots on the Hudson river,
and filled in by the corporation for sale. The Varick basin
lots had once been granted, but had been bought back and
filled in as already noted.

These sales, with six thousand five hundred and twenty dollars received for an isolated lot sold in 1816, aggregate two
hundred and twenty-six thousand dollars. Deducting twenty-
five per cent, to be paid to the sinking fund under the ordi-

[1] Map VIII.

[2] Ten acres of this land are shown on Map XVI between Sixty-third and Sixty-
fifth streets, Eighth and Ninth avenues.

[3] Map XIV, lots V–VIII inclusive.

[4] Map XI.

[5] Map X.

nance of 1813, leaves one hundred and seventy thousand dollars, or sufficient with the two hundred and twenty-five thousand dollars temporary loans and the two hundred thousand dollars stock to make up the four years' deficit of six hundred thousand dollars. Nevertheless the two hundred and twenty-five thousand dollars was still a debt, and to buy the ground for Fulton Market as much more was borrowed.[1] Increased taxation only met current expenses; the time was unfavorable for land sales; and those of 1818--19 had not escaped criticism, judging from the elaborate report of the comptroller in 1820, ordered to be printed for distribution and explaining and justifying the financial policy of the preceding four years. Accordingly four hundred thousand dollars' worth of five per cent. city stock, payable in 1850 and 1851, was issued; two hundred thousand dollars in July, 1820, and two hundred thousand dollars at three per cent. premium in May, 1821.

[1] "Acquired Jan. 12, 1821. Consideration $216,284.60." Comptroller's real estate index.

6. 1822-1843

STEADY CONSERVATION OF REMAINING MUNICIPAL LAND, WITH RESTRAINT OF DEBT TILL 1834, AFTER WHICH EXPENDITURE ON CROTON AQUEDUCT PREPARES THE WAY FOR THE POLICY OF 1844

There were now in reserve four hundred and eighty-four acres of the common land.   Between May, 1823, and January, 1827, four hundred and eighty acres of this would be available for sale.   It had been the expectation, and continued to be as late as 1823, that these lands would so enhance in value by the time the bulk of the six per cent. stock fell due, December 31st, 1826, that they might be sold to advantage and the stock taken up with the proceeds.   With this view the stock of 1812 had been made payable just after the bulk of existing leases would expire, and leases made thereafter had been limited to the same period.   The real estate market, however, continued too depressed between 1823 and 1827 to warrant sales of unimproved land, so that comparatively few of the five-acre lots were at this time parted with.   Of the ninety-three lots shown on Ludlam's atlas of 1821 as then belonging to the city, fifty-two were leased again, but only till 1833, at an average of thirty dollars each per year as against ten dollars in 1803; three were leased for twenty-one years; twelve or thirteen were held idle; as many more were worked by the almshouse; and twelve were sold in fee.

These were lots 115, 121 and 181 for four thousand dollars; lots 95, 89, 77 for two thousand five hundred dollars and a quit-rent commutation of four hundred dollars; lots 107, 109, 183 and 101 for four thousand five hundred dollars; lots 67 and 83, for one thousand five hundred dollars each, and a quit-rent.   In 1827, by exception, one of the fifty-two leased lots, namely, lot 110, "little more than a mass of rock," was also sold for two thousand five hundred and fifty dollars.

Since the sales of 1796 and 1801, the only interference with these lands had been by way of resale, exchange, or for exceptional reasons, as follows:

1802. Lot 119 to John Titus, he paying one hundred and fifty dollars and giving back to the city lot 128.

1804. Lots 54, 55, 60 and 61 to Dr. David Hosack for a botanic garden, price four thousand eight hundred and seven dollars and the usual wheat quit-rent.[1]

1804. Lot 80 with the usual reservation of a wheat quit-rent, for thirteen hundred and twenty dollars. This was one of the alternate lots marked to be sold in 1796, but was omitted from that sale and also from the resale of 1801.

1804. Lot 168, with the usual reservation of wheat quit-rent, for one thousand dollars.

1804. Lot 74, in the same way, for one thousand five hundred dollars.

1806. Lot 160, for nine hundred and forty dollars.

These three lots were of those sold in 1796 but not claimed, and were omitted from the resale of 1801. In 1796 they brought three hundred and thirty-five, one hundred and eighty-five and two hundred and forty pounds respectively, one pound being equivalent to two dollars and fifty cents.

1808. Lots 102 and 103 to the people of the state of New York, as already noted, for seven hundred dollars.

1808. Lot 110 reconveyed to the city for two thousand dollars, in order that the two hundred and fifty feet park-way through Hamilton square might be continued to Fifth avenue. In 1796 it sold for three hundred and five pounds, but was not

---

[1] Map V. Through the exertions of Dr. Hosack these were taken of him by the state under the law of 1810, and in 1814 given to Columbia College. They lie between Forty-seventh and Fifty-first streets, Fifth avenue and a line about one hundred feet east of Sixth avenue. The college still owns all the street lots and about one-fourth of those on the avenue. It has naturally received the attention of Single Tax advocates, one of whom, writing for their organ *The Standard*, estimates the value of the college lots to-day, perhaps too generously, at four million dollars.

claimed, and was resold in 1801 for four hundred and ninety dollars.

1809. Lot 205 sold for fifteen hundred and fourteen dollars. This lot was a portion of the tract east of Third avenue which was held back from the sale of 1796 at the request of adjacent owners and for the most part bought by them at a valuation fixed by the city. In 1809 the adjacent owner was allowed to purchase it at the valuation of 1796, namely one hundred and sixty pounds per acre.

1810. Lot 138 to James Scott, he paying two hundred dollars and reconveying to the city lot 137.

1810. Lot 84 reconveyed to the city by Dr. Hosack.

1818. Lots 125, 128, 131 to Robert Lenox, he reconveying to the city lots 167 and 169 which he held of the city on lease, and lots 166 and 168 which he owned in fee, and paying five hundred dollars.

1823. Lots 48 and 96 reconveyed to the city.

A like conservative policy was pursued in regard to the down-town lots. Most of them were on leases which expired in 1825, 1826 and 1827, and of all that belonged to the large tracts hitherto considered, only a few were sold between 1819 and 1840. The extension of Anthony street to Little Water cut the largest remaining gore of the Collect lots into eligible halves,[1] and these were sold in 1825, the one for one thousand three hundred and fifty dollars, the other for six hundred and thirty-nine dollars. The same year the western triangle of the powder-house lots fronting Pearl Street was sold for twenty-five hundred dollars. These were all of such lots that the city parted with until 1832, and then only two more were sold, namely, lot 4 of the powder house lots for two thousand five hundred dollars, and lot 5 for one thousand seven hundred and forty dollars. Another, the easternmost and last of the powder house lots, after Centre street had been opened through them, was sold in 1838 for five thousand dollars. This was all

[1] Map VIII.

again until 1840, although the extension of Collect street as
Centre street to Chatham, absorbed a number of corporation
lots on Tryon Row and Augustus street.[1]

The great bulk of these lots, as the leases fell in, were again
leased for twenty-one years. The advance in rents was general, though not quite uniform. The ruling rate for lots on
the south side of Chatham street in 1806 was two hundred
and fifty dollars, for those on the north side two hundred dollars. In 1827, lots 116 and 117 on the south side were leased
for four hundred and fifty dollars each and lots 2 and 6 on the
north side for four hundred dollars each. Lots on William
street which in 1806 rented for one hundred dollars were renewed in 1828 for one hundred and seventy-five dollars; num
bers 1 and 2 of the powder house lots which rented in
1811 for seventy-five dollars and one hundred and thirty-five
dollars, were renewed in 1832 for one hundred and seventy-
five dollars each, while numbers 4 and 5 adjacent were
sold the same year, as already noted, for two thousand five
hundred and one thousand seven hundred and forty dollars.
They had rented in 1811 for one hundred and fifty dollars and
one hundred dollars respectively.

Meanwhile the maturing six per cent. stock had to be provided for. From December, 1822, to December, 1825, the
floating debt had been slightly diminished to one hundred and
twelve thousand dollars, so that the normal increase of the
sinking fund was working an actual decrease of the debt. To
swell the fund and so reduce the amount inevitably to be
borrowed when the six per cents. fell due, all water lot quit-
rents, and not merely those from grants prior to January.
1804, were allowed in 1825 to be commuted, but at five per
cent. instead of six; and it was voted to carry to the sinking
fund all the proceeds of sales of corporation real estate
subsequent to January, 1825. From 1822 on, also, the new
Fulton market had returned a substantial sum .in fees and
rents. Even with these helps the sinking fund on the first of

[1] Map VIII.

January, 1826, was two hundred and twenty-five thousand dollars short of the seven hundred thousand dollars due the following December, though it exceeded by seventy-five thousand dollars Comptroller Mercein's estimate of 1812, and one hundred and thirty thousand dollars of it was in fives of 1820 and 1821.[1]   Resort was, therefore, had to temporary loans, and to retire the last of the six per cents., three hundred thousand dollars new fives payable in 1850 were issued in December, 1828, at 4½ per cent. premium, under the act of 1826.[2]

As early as 1826 the Bellevue establishment, "proud" though it had been termed in 1812, was already outgrown and unhealthy. The new state's prison at Sing Sing was then building, and it was thought that the old one at Greenwich, foot of Christopher street, might be made use of by the city. An agreement was therefore made with the state to take it on the completion of Sing Sing for one hundred thousand dollars. By the time the state was ready to give up possession, Blackwell's Island had been determined upon as the better site, and the purchase made in 1828 for thirty-two thousand five hundred dollars. Nevertheless the city held to its bargain for the prison property, borrowed the money to pay for it, and the next year, 1829, divided it into lots. Its extent was about six acres, including the wharf, and it made one hundred city lots.[3] These were sold at auction in April 1829, to thirty-six purchasers, for an aggregate of one hundred and twenty-eight thousand dollars. It was a profitable speculation, like that of the government house lots, rather than an administration of the city's proper estate, but it helped materially in the erection of the new penitentiary at Blackwell's Island, which was

[1] I have not found in any one place, a complete set of the comptroller's reports even for 1830 and after. Earlier reports were not printed as public documents. They occur, but not regularly, in the minutes of the common council. The comptroller's report for 1826, and with it the report of the sinking fund, are of those not entered.

[2] Comptroller's report 1830.

[3] Map XII.

pushed with such energy that the removal from Bellevue was
made in October, 1829. It was none too soon. An epidemic,
in which the eyesight of numbers of children was sacrificed,
broke out in the Almshouse in 1830, and forced the purchase
of Long Island farms, two hundred and fifty acres, at New-
town, and the removal of the children thither.

The ten years 1825 to 1835, as subsequent to the opening
of the Erie and Champlain Canals, were years of rapid growth
in wealth and population. Real estate increased from fifty-
two to one hundred and forty-two millions assessed value,[1]
population from one hundred and sixty-six thousand to two
hundred and seventy thousand. In correspondence with this
growth the great public work of the time, particularly after
1830, was the closing of many of the old streets and lanes
and the opening of new streets and avenues, as laid down by
the commissioners under the law of 1807. After Third avenue,
the first of the new streets to be opened[2] through the upper
commons was Forty-second street in 1831. In 1835 Seventh
avenue and Sixth avenue were opened; in 1836 Fifth, Madison
and Lexington avenues, the last two only to Forty-second
street; also Eighty-ninth, Ninetieth and Fiftieth streets from
Third to Sixth avenue, and Twenty-ninth to Forty-first inclusive.[3] The opening of cross-streets through the upper commons was much delayed by controversies which arose on
account of the new streets not coinciding with the streets
above Forty-second on the map by which the common lands
were sold in 1796. The map showed streets uniformly of sixty
feet wide, but the commissioners' map of 1813 made Forty-
second, Fifty-seventh, Seventy-second, Seventy-ninth and
Eighty-sixth streets one hundred feet wide, so that there was
overlapping of the new streets beyond the lines of the old ones,

[1] Proceedings of the Common Council, March, 1836.

[2] By opening is here meant the final determination of awards for land taken, not
the opening of a street for travel.

[3] Valentine's Manual for 1857, p. 529.

until above Seventy-ninth street the old lots were cut fairly in two.[1] With some of the owners the corporation arranged to give and take corresponding slips; with others no agreement could be reached until the law of 1836 gave to commissioners, "in all cases which may be submitted to them" the power to determine whether and what pieces should be mutually conveyed by the corporation and individuals, and on what terms. The next year the following streets were opened through the commons: Forty-third to Fifty-seventh and Eighty-seventh to Eighty-eighth inclusive; and from Eighty-third to Eighty-fifth inclusive, between Third and Fifth avenues.

Probably on account of this uncertainty over boundaries, only five of the fifty-two lots, the leases of which expired in 1833, were leased again in that year, though meanwhile two others had been leased for twenty-one years in 1832. After 1833 and until 1842 only six more were leased, none of them longer than to 1846. Beginning with 1842 the lots were let out in bulk from year to year in anticipation of sales on account of the sinking fund. Not one had been sold since 1827.

The sales on account of the sinking fund, which began on a large scale in the year 1844, were resolved upon in consequence of fiscal conditions hitherto unknown to the city. These, again, were the outcome of an undertaking really vast for that time, the Croton Aqueduct. For forty years previous to 1835 it had been a mooted question whence a supply of water was to be obtained for the New York of the future. Several large schemes had been brought forward and abandoned. Begun at last in 1835, with the expectation that it would cost five millions, the Croton Aqueduct was not finished until 1845, after an expenditure of thirteen millions. It was accompanied by a series of smaller undertakings which in themselves were sufficient to absorb the accumulations of the sinking fund and any surplus after other expenses were met. Accordingly the city debt, which in December, 1834, was, all

[1] Maps V and VI.

together, seven hundred and forty-five thousand dollars, had increased by December, 1843, to thirteen million six hundred and seventy-five thousand one hundred and thirty-four dollars. These minor extraordinary expenditures were principally for:

The Tombs, fifty-nine thousand dollars in 1835, two hundred and sixty-one thousand five hundred dollars in 1837.

Randall's Island, 1835, sixty thousand dollars.

Ground for markets, 1835, thirty-eight thousand nine hundred and fifty dollars.

Lumber Dock, 1835, twelve thousand dollars; 1837, sixty thousand dollars.

Lunatic Asylum, 1837, sixty thousand dollars.

In addition, the city was obliged to pay three hundred and sixty thousand dollars damages for blowing up buildings to stop the great fire of December, 1835. Other expenditures which swelled the debt, but only to furnish later the means to diminish it, were:

Fifty-three thousand dollars, 1834–1835, for filling in one hundred lots at Bellevue.

Twenty-seven thousand seven hundred and sixty dollars in 1834–1835, for filling in forty lots at Fort Gansevoort.

The current funds for this outlay were obtained by the issue of five hundred thousand dollars building stock in 1837–1838; and of three hundred and sixty thousand dollars fire indemnity stock; and by temporary loans which in 1840 were funded to the amount of four hundred thousand dollars. The water stock outstanding December, 1843, was twelve million two hundred thousand dollars. On eight hundred thousand dollars of it issued in 1842, the city was obliged to pay seven per cent. interest. It was clear that its credit was suffering under the load, and needed more adequate provision for paying so great a debt as it should mature. Under these circumstances the ordinance of 1844 was passed. The important seventeenth section is as follows: " The commissioners of the sinking fund are hereby authorized to sell and dispose of

all real estate belonging to the corporation and not in use for
or reserved for public purposes, at public auction, at such time
and on such terms as they may deem most advantageous for
the public interest; provided, however, that no property shall be
disposed of for a smaller sum than that affixed to the description of such property, under title fifth of this ordinance; and
that at least twenty days' previous notice of the time and place
of such sale, including a description of the property to be
sold, be published in each of the newspapers employed by the
Corporation."

Under this ordinance what was left of corporation land not
used for public purposes passed into the control of the commissioners of the sinking fund, in trust expressly for the payment of the city debt. The bulk of this residue, not counting
Long Island Farms, lay in the upper and lower commons and
at Bellevue, with smaller but valuable blocks, where there
had been reservation of water-lot grants, at Duane, King and
Gansevoort streets on the North river, and at Peck slip, and
Munroe market on the East river. On Map XVI., the shaded
part shows the remaining corporation lots north of Forty-
second street. Below Forty-second street were still forty-five
acres of the upper commons, as may be seen on Map V.[1] Of
the lower commons there remained more than half the original lots left after the settlement of boundary disputes.[2] The
Bellevue establishment had been entirely removed to the
islands, leaving there two hundred and eighty-three eligible
city lots,[3] and there were seven still left at Peck slip. Of the
King and West street block only one lot out of twenty-six
had been sold.[4] The Duane, Gansevoort and Stanton street
or Munroe market lots were not yet productive, and need
only be named.

[1] Lots 16, 17, 18, 21, 22, 25, 26, 31, 32, 33.
[2] Map XIV. The lots sold are shaded.
[3] Map XV.
[4] Map XIII.

After more than a century and a half, therefore, the city still had left, besides the Bellevue property acquired by purchase, no inconsiderable portion of the estate above high water mark received under the Dongan Charter. The estate in its various parcels as heretofore referred to, and including the Harlem commons, comprised more than one-seventh of the whole upland, including its choicest part.[1]

Previous to the ordinance of 1844, the disposition of the city property had rested solely with the common council, which carried its resolves into effect generally through the agency of its finance committee; in routine matters, of its treasurer; and. later of its comptroller, first appointed in 1802. The comptroller's reports and recommendations were customarily referred to the finance committee, on whose advice, on the comptroller's or its own motion, the board passed its resolves. By the charter of 1830 the assistant aldermen were made a separate chamber and the mayor was given a veto which, however, could be overruled by a majority vote in each chamber. Measures could originate in either chamber, and took effect on a majority vote in each, followed by the Mayor's approval or ten days' inaction. There was no restraint on alienation in any way the common council might choose. After the ordinance of 1844, the common council confined itself to directing special conveyances, sometimes to individuals or corporate bodies, at prices to be fixed by the commissioners of the sinking fund, sometimes to institutions gratuitously.

The sinking fund commission used its new powers vigorously, and by large sales, principally in 1844, 1845, 1848, 1850, 1851, 1852, 1857, 1866, converted the greater part of the estate intrusted to it into current funds, and applied them to reduce

---

[1] The present acreage of the island is given at the tax commissioners' office as twelve thousand four hundred and thirty-two: but of this about two thousand four hundred acres have been filled out into the rivers. The parcels heretofore referred to and not including water lots aggregate one thousand four hundred. and fifty acres, one thousand six hundred and fifty and over if probable encroachments be reckoned.

the debt. The sales-maps and accounts are on file in the comptroller's office,[1] and with the comptroller's reports and contemporaneous records of the common council, constitute the chief material for continuing this account to the present time.

The story of the sales between those already described and those by the commissioners is soon told, so far as concerns the larger blocks to which this account is confined. Few and, except in one case, unimportant, they are here referred to only that a complete view may be had of the disposal of the parcels to which they belong. The special circumstances attending each sale have not been inquired into, so that a tabular statement merely is subjoined. It will at least go to show that the city record of transactions in common land is complete and accounts fully and properly for all there was to dispose of.

1840. A Peck slip lot, west corner of Front street, fifty-five by twenty five, to lessee, eight thousand dollars. It had been leased in 1828 for twenty-one years at three hundred and seventy-five dollars yearly.

1841. At Albany basin, a strip seventy-eight feet deep, in west front of the lots sold in 1818,[2] forty-six thousand two hundred and fifty dollars.

1842. A Collect lot, No. 1, twenty-five by ninety, corner of Elm and Leonard streets, four thousand eight hundred dollars.[3] The lot fifty feet by forty on southwest corner opposite sold in 1805 for six hundred dollars.

1842. The first of a hitherto intact block of twenty-five lots bounded by King, Charlton, Washington and West streets. It had been reserved in granting the water lots, and was the fifth block along the North river, which the corporation had

[1] To the courtesy of Comptroller Myers, I am indebted for the opportunity of ample access to the maps and records in his office.

[2] Map XI.

[3] Map VIII.

filled in for sale.[1]   It was leased in 1837 for ten years at four thousand and fifty dollars annually.   Price of the one lot, thirty feet by seventy, five thousand six hundred dollars.

1842.   Lower commons, lot 20, as on Map XIV., three thousand five hundred dollars.

1843.   Lower commons, lot 6, eight thousand five hundred dollars.   Leased in 1825 for twenty-one years at five hundred dollars yearly.

This brings us to the sales by the commissioners of the sinking fund.

[1] Map XIII.

CHAPTER III

ENCROACHMENTS

IN the history of municipal land ownership, as is well known, encroachments are conspicuous. To what extent have they been made on Manhattan Island? The limiting words of the Charter of 1686 are "all vacant, waste and unpatented lands." It was from the start the practice of the common council in any case of suspected encroachment to require a view of the patent under which the land was held, and to claim so much as it did not cover to be the property of the city. Several instances have already been noted where claimants of ground between low and high water were summoned to show title by their patents. So it was with the upland. In the case of a tract at the junction of the Post and Bloomingdale roads, shown on Goerck's map[1] as belonging to Casper Semler, the patent under which it was held was demanded as late as 1757, and on its appearing that the patent gave one hundred rods along the Post road and fifty rods back, while by an error of an early surveyor fifty rods had been taken on the road, and one hundred rods back, a settlement was entered on the minutes of the common council whereby the occupant retained his ground as it was, save a gore which he gave up not to overrun the Bloomingdale road, receiving an equivalent gore in return.

By laying down correctly the original patents, up to 1686, the lines of the city's property could be accurately determined. This, however, was not practicable below Wall street, as Valentine's attempt has shown. From Wall street

[1] Map V.

as far north as the junction of the Post and Bloomingdale
roads, except the shore, the common council seem not to have
succeeded in their attempts to reclaim ground already in oc-
cupancy, and even that which they gave to Sir Peter Warren
on Broadway, though unoccupied, was contested by an adjacent owner.   Above the junction to the Harlem line the patents are large and well defined, and there can be little doubt
what the city ought to have received under the Charter, ad-
mitting its right, which does not seem to have been gainsaid,
to all unpatented land.   On the east the Harlem line, as set
forth in the Nichols patent of 1666, is a definite boundary.
The controversy with Harlem freeholders over their indefinite right of commonage west of it, and its outcome, have
already been noted.   Beginning at the Harlem line, the western boundary of the commons is for some distance the eastern
line of Theunis Ide's land, run in 1690, the town of Harlem
paying for part of the survey.   This line extended from One
hundred and seventh to Eighty-ninth street, about half way between Seventh and Eighth avenues.[1]   It does not seem to have
been questioned by the city of New York, though I find no
mention of the patent under which it was held.

   South of Ide's land a single patent extends to Thirty-ninth
street, on the river to Forty-second, "from the said river
stretching in depth and breadth two hundred and fifty rods."
A line at all points two hundred and fifty rods inland from
Hudson high water mark, as shown in Randel's maps, would
fall half a block, on an average, short of the commons line, as
held by the city, from Eighty-ninth to Seventy-first streets,
and indicates an encroachment of that extent.   From Seventy-
first to Sixty-fourth streets the two lines would nearly co-
incide.   From Sixty-fourth to Fifty-fifth the apparent encroachment would be about one block or eight hundred feet
against the city, and a block and a half against the city from
Fifty-fifth to Forty-third street.   Below Forty-third street the

[1] Map II.   Compare Map XVI.

Bloomingdale road is the actual and apparently the true line of the commons. This calculation would show a possible encroachment of say one hundred and eighty-five acres into the common on the west, south of Theunis Ide's land. The common council does not seem to have been aware that two miles and a half along the Hudson and bordering the commons were held under the same patent, but appears to have taken contemporaneous deeds as conclusive.[1] Thus there is record of an agreement in 1749 with Oliver de Lancy, holder or co-holder under the patent through several mesne conveyances of the tract west of the commons from Fifty seventh to Sixty-eighth streets, whereby he is to have his land surveyed and pay three pounds an acre for any he may possess that properly belongs to the commons. A committee made the survey and the deed was ordered, though it does not seem to have passed, but no mention was made of an original patent.

On the east side, the line of the commons for the greater part of its length was kept quite rigorously up to the true line of the patents. Tuttle's maps show scarcely any discrepancy from Seventy-eighth street, where the commons ranging along the Harlem line would first touch the rear of the East river patents, as far as Sixty-seventh street. From Sixty sixth to Forty-eighth street they indicate an encroachment varying from one hundred and fifty to five hundred feet. Below Forty-eighth street to the Bloomingdale road, the old post road is either approximately or exactly the limit of the patents, and there is no encroachment beyond it. Minutes of controversies

---

[1] The early deeds cite the patent and give the distance from the river as two hundred and fifty rods. Joseph Haynes, who held the southmost fifth of the patent at his death in 1763, occupied only two hundred and fifty rods, or to the Bloomingdale road, from Thirty ninth to Forty ninth streets, and he had his land surveyed by the city surveyor in 1760. See 42 Conveyances, p. 49. For the tract north of him to the De Lancy line, deeds recorded in 1727 and 1761 give two hundred and fifty rods only. See "Tuttle's Abstract of Farm Titles in the City of New York," p. 200 and p. 329. Tuttle is mistaken in saying, p. 46, that the deed to Joseph Haynes gives distances which would extend his tract east of the Bloomingdale road. See 42 Conveyances, p. 27.

with owners all along the East river side of the commons occur frequently in the records of the common council previous to 1790. In some cases a survey showed that land uninclosed was really within a patent; in others land was given up by private occupants, ten acres by three different persons in 1773.[1] The six-acre lot and the one-acre lot shown in Goerck's map were sold by the city to the holders in 1792. Subtracting these from the amount of possible encroachments as shown by Tuttle's map, would leave approximately thirty-five acres as the probable loss to the city on the east side. Two hundred and twenty acres then is the upward limit of encroachments on the whole upper commons, or about one-sixth of the un-patented land there.

In the vicinity of the lower commons the city was itself the encroacher and was obliged to relinquish, as has been noted, portions of the negroes' burying ground and certain lots adjacent.

An attempt was made in 1758–60 to assert the city's title to portions of a large tract surrounded by the Bowery lane and Bloomingdale road, the cross road leading thence to Great Kills, the road from Great Kills to Greenwich lane, and the Greenwich lane in its extent from the Great Kills road to the Bowery lane. Bowery lane is the Bowery; the Bloomingdale road its continuation in Broadway; the creek called Great Kills was the southern boundary of the eight hundred rods patent already referred to; the road from Great Kills to Greenwich lane, known as the Fitzroy road, followed approximately the line of Eighth avenue from the cross road to Greenwich lane, the Greenwich avenue of to-day, which was then continued to the Bowery at Astor Place; the cross road met the Bloomingdale road at Thirty-ninth street, and the Fitzroy road at

[1] Litigation over the division line on the east side from Forty-eighth to Fifty-seventh street was begun in 1838 and continued until 1867, when the city paid eighty-four thousand four hundred and nineteen dollars for a quit-claim deed fixing the line there as in Map XVI. Comptroller's report, 1845, p. 35; and 992 Conveyances, p. 536.

[2] Map III.

Forty-second street.[1] In the common council minutes of July, 1760, there is an elaborate report in regard to the ownership of this tract, and there is described "a large central vacancy, but how far, for want of further discoveries which can only be made by tedious researches after old patents in the secretary's office, or whether the same extends quite to Greenwich lane, we cannot as yet say—which vacancy, from what we have hitherto discovered, is occasioned by two tiers of patents, the rears of which do not meet each other. How this vacancy came to be left out of the adjoining patents we think is easily determinable if it be considered that the aforesaid vacancy is an entire swamp, which sort of land it is well known was not anciently esteemed worth patenting." The committee were instructed to sell or lease what encroachments they found on a closer survey, as they should think best. It is possible that patents were found covering the whole of the tract, since there is no later record of conveyances. The incident shows the usual procedure of the corporation in ascertaining what lands it owned under the Dongan Charter. The custom was to claim all uninclosed land until patents were produced for it. Where there was suspicion that inclosed land was so by encroachment the usual practice was to demand a view of the occupant's patent. There is no record of any attempt systematically to ascertain the lands to which the city was entitled by its charter, by compiling the original grants in the secretary's office. Hoffman has done this below the line of Houston street, the Bowery, and Greenwich lane, to Wall street and Battery Place. Tuttle and Riker show it from Thirty-ninth street up. The intervening tract in which the "vacancy" just described lies has not yet been accounted for to the extent of citing and plotting out the original patents.

[1] This tract is shown in relation to present streets and avenues on the map that faces p. 379 of Valentine's History of the City of New York.

CHAPTER IV

GRANTS TO INSTITUTIONS AND CORPORATIONS

ANOTHER matter like that of encroachments at all times of interest in the history of municipal landownership, is that of grants to institutions and corporations. The list of such grants of upland on Manhattan Island down to 1844 is as follows:

1691. Dutch Church. Lot one hundred and eighty feet by eighty-four on Garden street, now Exchange Place, for a church or for pious and charitable uses. Consideration fifty-four pounds.

1703. English or Trinity Church. "The new burying ground three hundred and ten feet front on Broadway, to be used as a church yard and burial place forever." Consideration nominal.

1766. Reformed Protestant Dutch Church. Twenty-eight lots of lower commons, the same not to be converted forever after to private uses. Perpetual lease, rent seventy pounds annually. Condition released for one thousand pounds in 1790.

1766. English Presbyterian Church. Block now occupied by Times and Potter buildings, not to be applied to private or secular uses. Perpetual lease, rent forty pounds annually, reduced to twenty-one pounds and five shillings on petition in 1785. Condition released in 1856, the city receiving sixty-seven thousand five hundred dollars.

1797. People of the State of New York. Two acres at junction of Post and Bloomingdale roads for the use of an arsenal, to revert to the city when abandoned for said purpose. Consideration nominal. The state made no use of the property. By act of legislature it was restored to the city, and in 1807 granted to the United States on similar terms.

1808. People of the State of New York. Lots 102 and 103 common lands. In 102 the city had a right only to a wheat quit-rent. Lot 103 was on lease which would expire in 1823. For its whole interest the city received seven hundred dollars. The arsenal building erected by the state still stands in Central Park.

1808. Free school society. Free use and occupation of building forty feet by one hundred and nineteen, corner of Chatham street and Tryon row, and of its site as shown in Map VIII. The lot is described as the arsenal site on Tryon row released by the State of New York to the corporation. Condition to occupy the premises for the uses of the institution, and to educate gratuitously the children belonging to the city almshouse.

1808. People of the State of New York. Collect lots north of Sugar Loaf street, and between present Centre and Elm,[1] one square and part of another, for arsenal, laboratory, work shops and ordnance yard, so long as the same should be used for military purposes and no longer. Consideration nominal.

1810. Manumission society. Lots 107 and 161 William street,[2] in trust for school purposes, with condition to build within a limited time. The lots were on leases which the school bought in, and then the corporation remitted the rent. Consideration nominal.

1810. Trustees Brick Presbyterian Church. Lot 21 Augustus street, for charity school, otherwise to revert. The trustees failing to build in three years, as conditioned, were granted an extension till after the war. In 1816 their petition "to erect buildings ornamental to the city and profitable to the church" was refused and the lot re-entered.

1824. Society for reformation of juvenile delinquents. One

[1] Map VIII.
[2] Map IV.

acre in front of the United States arsenal grounds, junction of Post and Bloomingdale roads,[1] and the city's interest in said grounds, for a house of refuge for juvenile delinquents, on condition that the society obtain a conveyance from the United States of its interest in the premises, both lot and buildings, and that these shall at all times be used for said house of refuge. Fifth avenue was afterwards opened through the premises, on which account, in 1837, the society was given a lease of five hundred feet in depth of the block between Twenty-third and Twenty-fourth streets, First avenue and Avenue A, with the buildings thereon, being the old fever hospital of the Bellevue establishment, on condition that it execute a release to the city of its former premises and use the new site for no other purposes than those for which the society was incorporated.

1827. Institution for the instruction of the deaf and dumb. One acre of lot 59, common lands, in fee, consideration nominal. The institution had received ten thousand dollars from the state and a lease of the whole of lot 59 from the city for twenty-one years, at seventy-five dollars for the first fifteen years and one hundred dollars thereafter. Under the act granting the ten thousand dollars, the state comptroller refused to accept leased grounds as a site, whence the grant in fee of one acre. The institution held other portions of lot 59 and also part of lot 56 under various leases till 1850, when, by the direction of the common council, the sinking fund commission sold it both lots, except the one acre already conveyed, for twenty-eight thousand dollars.[2]

1828. New York Dispensary. Lot fifty feet by ninety of the state ordnance yard, corner Centre and White streets.[3] The legislature had released this parcel to the city to be so conveyed. The widening of Centre street took twenty feet off

---

[1] Map VII.
[2] Map XVI.
[3] Map VIII.

one side of the lot, which was added on the other in 1837 by grant of the state and city, as in 1828.

1830. Northern Dispensary. Triangle, fifty-one feet by seventy-two by sixty-two, Sixth street, near Christopher street; so long as used for the purposes of the dispensary. Consideration nominal.   .

1842. Association for the benefit of colored orphans in New York City; two hundred and fifty feet in depth from Fifth avenue of lot forty-two, common lands, upon condition to build in three years and to maintain twelve colored pauper children from the city almshouse, if so required; the inmates to be taken from and to belong to the city. Consideration nominal. In 1848, when the commissioners of the sinking fund sold the rest of the block at auction, the Association bought four city lots for two thousand and ninety dollars, thus extending its premises to a depth of three hundred feet from Fifth Avenue. In the draft riots of July, 1863, its building, which had cost about seven thousand dollars, was burned down. For this and other losses it then suffered, the Association received from the city seventy-three thousand dollars. In 1865 it sold its land for one hundred and seventy thousand dollars. New grounds were purchased at One hundred and forty-third street and Tenth avenue for forty-five thousand dollars, and the large building that now stands there was erected.

CHAPTER V

COMMENT AND CONTROVERSY

THE reflection is unavoidable whether this vast property had been administered up to 1844 with a fair regard to the city's interest, even from a practical point of view; that is, from the standpoint not of what would have been best, but what was well. Passing over an apparent apathy as to encroachments on the west side and into the "large central vacancy" of 1760, for lack of data as to what certainly took place there, the most questionable transactions from such a standpoint are the sales of 1789 and 1792,[1] when two hundred and forty acres of the commons, equal to forty-eight full city blocks, were sold in bulk as farm land to ten purchasers at less than sixty-five dollars per acre. These sales were not up to the standard of either earlier or later administrations. To be sure the nearest of this land was three miles from the city, but the city had over thirty thousand people, an increase of at least thirty per cent. in three years. The only excuse seems to be a natural anxiety to recoup losses after a long war. After these sales till 1844, with minor exceptions again after the war, the administration of this public trust was conservative and judicious. The policy adopted in 1796 of selling alternate sections of the commons and holding on to the rest, was carried out faithfully, and the rise in value of the unsold lots was awaited for fifty years. In selling the Collect lots one full square, the site of the Tombs, was reserved to the city; and a square and a half was granted to the State under such conditions that it is available for municipal purposes to-day, saving the city at least a million of dollars in the cost of its new crim-

[1] These are the dates of the contracts, not of the deeds.

inal courts building. The authorities were even sharp specu-
lators for the city's interests in the purchase and sale of the
government house and state's prison lots. The proceeds of
sales were not dissipated in current expenses, but were used
directly or through the sinking fund to pay for permanent
improvements.

If the standpoint be changed, and it is asked what disposition
of these acres would have been the best possible for the permanent welfare of the city, the question becomes one of theory,
and there will be various answers. Some stock arguments
against municipal ownership are not borne out by the city's
experience. Up to 1844 there had been neither a dishonest nor
a fickle administration of the municipal estate. Governments,
parties and officials changed, but there is a distinct continuity
of fiscal policy, so far at least as relates to corporation land.
It would seem that underneath the tossing surface of politics
there were deep economic interests of which political dynasties
are the servants and not the masters, and which secure the re-
tention to old age of not a few experienced officials, even under a system by which the spoils belong to the victors.

On the other hand, the contention that municipal ownership and the leasehold system made necessary by it are rela-
tively unprofitable, and unfavorable to improvements, is sus-
tained. Improvements would hardly be undertaken on a
shorter lease than twenty-one years, and on its twenty-one
year leases as sold at auction the city got no fair return on
the average selling value of its property for that time.[1] Neither
were the structures put up creditable. Nearly all were but
two story and attic brick buildings, the minimum required
by the leases.

In new communities at least, private ownership in fee seems
to be required to encourage improvement, and so far as it does
encourage it, benefits the community generally. Were we com-

[1] There is considerable evidence for this statement in the prices and rentals
heretofore quoted. The revenue items in Table B are to the same effect.

mon owners again of the ground under the Potter and Times buildings, and it stood vacant, it would be better policy to give it to men who would put up those buildings than to rent it to others who would improve it in the ordinary way. Every branch of trade and many classes of workers would share in the benefit. Exclusive private ownership has this advantage, that under the stress of its competition those who are in general best able to improve the land get it. It is also true that some of these, thanks to the practice of assessing vacant lots for purposes of taxation lower than improved property of the same value, find it more congenial not to use their power, and buy merely to sell again, or for various causes do not half utilize their holdings. This is the vice of the system, but it is a curable one.

Already there is in New York City, for example, perceptibly less favoring of vacant lots in making up the tax list; and it is to be expected that such favoritism, inherited from a time when municipal taxes and expenditures were comparatively insignificant, will not last much longer. To tax them an extra fifteenth, as Stuyvesant once did, would no doubt be crude treatment, but certainly not worse adapted to present conditions than the bounty now in effect extended to them as compared with improved property. It is a familiar conception that nothing economic is so beneficial to a community as to have every one at work and utilization everywhere. When this conception dominates taxation so that utilities are not discouraged nor non-utilization encouraged, the real merits of private ownership of land will be much more apparent; and they are poor defenders of it who in the case of city land still stand by the old notion (harmless enough when local taxes were low, land cheap, and every one had already more work than he could do) that because valuable land is held idle, for that very reason it should be exempt or taxed at a minimum valuation, but that the moment it is improved and so begins to do some good, both it and the improvements may be assessed at the maximum valuation, from sixty to one hundred per cent. of selling value according to local custom.

If the view be correct that highest practical utilization carries with it greatest general benefit, and if the observation can be relied on that ownership by one and utilization by another do not conduce to a high grade of the latter, then both the leasehold and the speculative policy which were prevalent prior to 1844 must be considered less rational than the policy then inaugurated of getting the land into the hands of individuals and recouping through the increase of taxable property.

The chief consideration urged for municipal ownership of at least the suburban part of city land, is that thereby the community would profit by the increment due to its own growth and to improvements at its expense, whereas now private individuals grow rich without labor by selling to others as it were their place in the line. This "whereas" ignores the controlling fact that the man who has just sold his place in most cases paid a fair price for it to somebody before him, and therefore cannot be considered as having got something for nothing; it also takes no account of the effect to be expected from ceasing to favor vacant land on the tax list. The other part of the consideration adduced must be weighed against the doctrine of assessments. Ever since the law of 1691, this doctrine has prevailed in New York City. Beginning with 1787, one law after another has added to the list of betterments, the cost of which shall be met by assessments on properties benefited, until now even the cost of setting out trees along an avenue is so assessed.[1] The constitutionality of such laws was firmly

---

[1] The assessment for planting trees on West End avenue, from Seventy third to One Hundred and Seventh street, was twenty-two thousand two hundred and eighty dollars. For the developed assessment system of New York City, see the consolidation act of 1882, and amendments, Ash's 1891 Edition. For list of laws that mark the stages to that act, see Gerard. That the system like every other governmental power may be abused, the experience of 1870-1880 proves. From a statement presented by John Kelly, comptroller, to the assessment commission under the law of 1880, it appears that there were due the city April 30th, 1880, eight and one-half millions unpaid assessments. Eight and one third millions of

held in decisions of 1831 and 1851 by the state court of last resort.[1]

In the latter case Ruggles, J., said: " The attempt was made in the Convention of 1846 to abolish this mode of taxation. A standing committee was appointed to consider and report on the organization and power of cities and incorporated villages, and especially on their power of taxation, assessment, borrowing money, contracting debts, and loaning their credit. The majority of the committee reported in favor of prohibiting local assessment for any improvements in a city or village unless on application of the majority of the owners of the lands assessed, and unless upon a two-thirds vote of the Common Council or board of trustees. The minority reported this section: 'No assessment for any improvements in any city or village shall be laid otherwise than by a general tax upon the taxable property of such city or village, levied and collected with an annual tax for other expenses.' Debates in Convention, Argus Edition, p. 357. Both propositions failed, and the ninth section of the eighth article of the Constitution was substituted and adopted instead. The Constitution in this section recognizes and affirms the validity of the legislation by which city and village assessments for local purposes like that now in controversy are authorized; and seems to remove all doubt in relation to the legislative power in question."

such arrears had been allowed to accumulate in the years 1870–1879 inclusive, on assessments aggregating twenty-five and one-fourth millions, of which also two and one-half millions had been vacated by the courts, making a deficit of nearly eleven millions in ten years. This state of affairs was a legacy from the Tweed regime, which coming effectually into power in 1869 projected vast and premature improvements, and by extravagance and fraud in various directions was chiefly instrumental in piling up the city debt from thirty-six millions in January, 1869, to a maximum of one hundred and twenty millions in December, 1876.

[1] The Mayor, etc., of New York *vs.* Livingston (8 Wend., 85), and The People *vs.* The Mayor, etc., of Brooklyn (4 Comstock, 419). For a complete study of the subject the reader is now referred to Rosewater, *Special Assessments*, in the Columbia University Series in History, Economics and Public Law, Vol. II., No. 3.

Since, in virtue of the principle of assessment and the principle of the law of 1807, a map can be made one hundred years in advance of a growing city; individuals warned that no compensation will be granted them for buildings put within street lines; the lands in the streets taken by right of eminent domain as fast as the growth of the city demands; the amount paid for them, and the entire cost of regulating, sewering and paving recovered by benefit assessments, the city paying assessments on its property the same as private owners:—it may fairly be questioned what more efficient system is possible, or what present injustice connected with private ownership of land in cities would remain to be remedied, were this system fully utilized and supplemented by an equal treatment of the owners of vacant and improved lots in the matter of taxation. Compared to the possibilities of municipal ownership with its buying and holding, and leasing or selling again after improvements made, the process just described, which differs only in degree from that even now followed in New York City, seems like the clearing-house system in banking, compared with the old-time operations of non-clearing-house finance.

APPENDIX A

TABLE A

August 21, 1820, the Finance Committee, preparatory to opening the Comptroller's books on a new system, report an inventory in full of city property, which, if arranged under the same heads as in Table B., stands as follows:

AVAILABLE FOR PURPOSES OF SALE

Houses and lots, productive	$405,200
Productive property at Brooklyn	62,150
Common lands, productive	119,150
Common lands, unproductive	37,800
Common lands, rent payable in wheat	2,650
Common lands, on perpetual lease, rent in coin	1,260
City lots, rent payable in wheat	5,200
Total	$633,410

UNAVAILABLE FOR PURPOSES OF SALE

Public wharves, piers and slips	$842,257
Ferries, including necessary wharves	122,000
Lands and buildings used for public purposes	1,769,536
Total	$2,733,793

The assessed valuation of other real estate the same year was $52,063,858.

TABLE B

Recapitulation of the real estate belonging to the City of New York, with the valuation thereof and the revenue derived therefrom, as submitted to the City Convention, in the year 1846, by John Ewen, Comptroller. Documents of the City Convention, p. 132.

AVAILABLE FOR PURPOSES OF SALE

		Revenue.
Real estate for redemption of fire loan stock . . .	$127,718.55	$7,984.00
Bonds and mortgages pledged for redemption of fire loan stock	124,942.71	8,745.98
Quit-rents, water grants, bonds and mortgages. . .	591,931.27	25,740.91
Sundry lots and gores	246,540.00	
City lots under lease without covenants for renewal.	80,000.00	3,097.50
Miscellaneous property and rents in public buildings.	60,000.00	6,595.00
Lots at Brooklyn under lease without covenants for renewal	34,050.00	1,679.49
City lots under lease with covenants for renewal .	271,000.00	8,741.25
Common lands	1,078,500.00	1,606.74
Total	$2,614,682.53	$64,190.87

UNAVAILABLE FOR PURPOSES OF SALE

Real estate in use by fire department	$80,600.00	$1,005.00
Real estate in use for market purposes	1,116,000.00	52,990.93
Piers and wharves in use for general purposes . .	1,472,300.00	73,782.00
Piers and wharves in use for ferry purposes . . .	224,500.00	51,695.00
Real estate in use for school purposes, land . . .	90,950.00	
Real estate in use for school purposes, building . .	128,547.68	
Public parks and grounds	1,235,000.00	
Real estate in permanent use for city purposes . .	18,121,000.00	223,882.97
Total	$22,468.397.68	$403,355.90

The assessed value of other real estate the same year was $183,480,534.00. More than half the value of the entire cor- poration property centered in the Croton Aqueduct, then just completed, and it is Croton water rent that makes up nearly all the last item of revenue.

TABLE C

In the Comptroller's report for 1855 is a statement of the real estate then belonging to the city.   Arranged as in Tables A and B, it is as follows :

AVAILABLE FOR PURPOSES OF SALE

Lots under lease	$797,000
Sundry lots and gores	704,600
Lots at Brooklyn	15,000
Common lands	523,000
Uncommuted quit-rents and water grants yet to be issued	460,000
Total	$2,499,600

UNAVAILABLE FOR PURPOSES OF SALE

Almshouse department, including Blackwell's Island and buildings .	$1,700,000
Croton Aqueduct department	15,474,000
Police department	172,000
Fire department	298,000
Education department	1,555,800
Markets	1,176,000
Parks	13,984,369
Ferries	1,617,000
Piers and bulkheads	4,206,000
Total	$40,183,169

The assessed valuation of other real estate the same year was $336,975,866.

APPENDIX B.

THE accompanying maps were photo-engraved from tracings of originals as follows:

I. Fac-simile of Lynes' map of 1728. In the tracing, details of an ornamental nature, as also ward lines and names, were omitted, and a number of lots referred to in the text designated by reference marks. See also note on page 14.

II. Map accompanying Riker's History of Harlem. Used by permission of his widow. In the tracing, Central Park line was added, the Harlem line and road lettered, and some details omitted.

V. and VI. Goerck's map of 1796, in Comptroller's office. On the tracings were put additional memoranda of sale and exchange, with all dates and prices; also the lines of Third, Lexington and Seventh avenues, and of Fifth avenue below Forty-second street, and the intersection of present streets with the Middle road, now Fifth avenue. The lettering of other features departs from the original in type but not in effect.

VII. Holmes' Map No. 1, of Common Lands. Used by permission of B. S. Demarest. Much of the finer detail is omitted.

The others are on file in the Comptroller's office. Occasionally a word or mark has been added in the tracing to facilitate reference.

Map 1

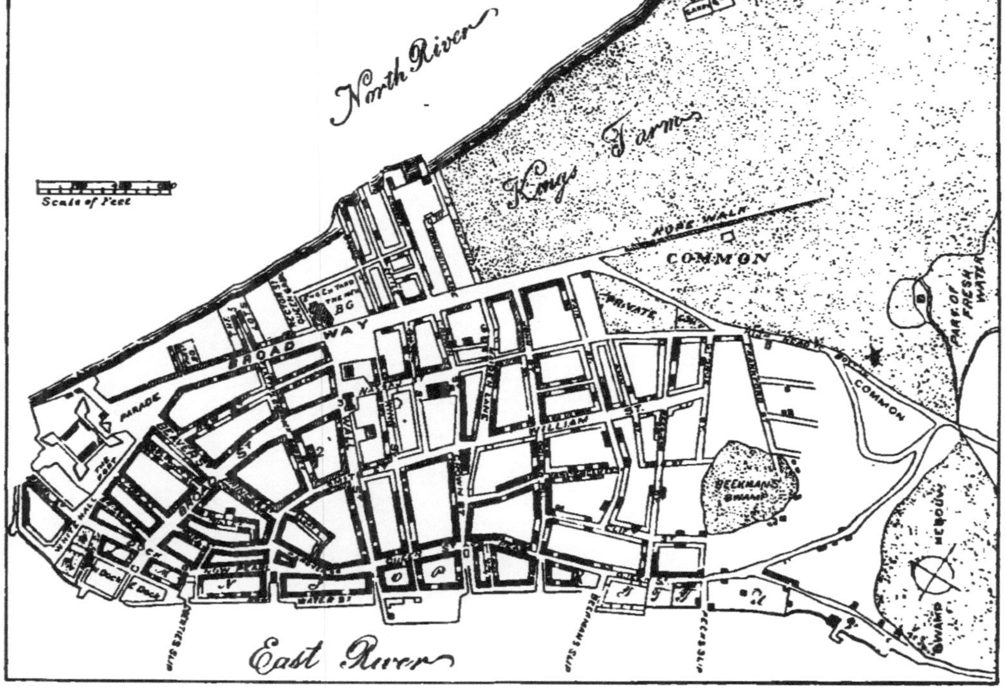

PART OF FRESH WATER

SWAMP

MEADOW

COMMON

North River

East River

BROADWAY

PECK'S SLIP

BEEKMAN'S SLIP

COUNTIES SLIP

Scale of Feet

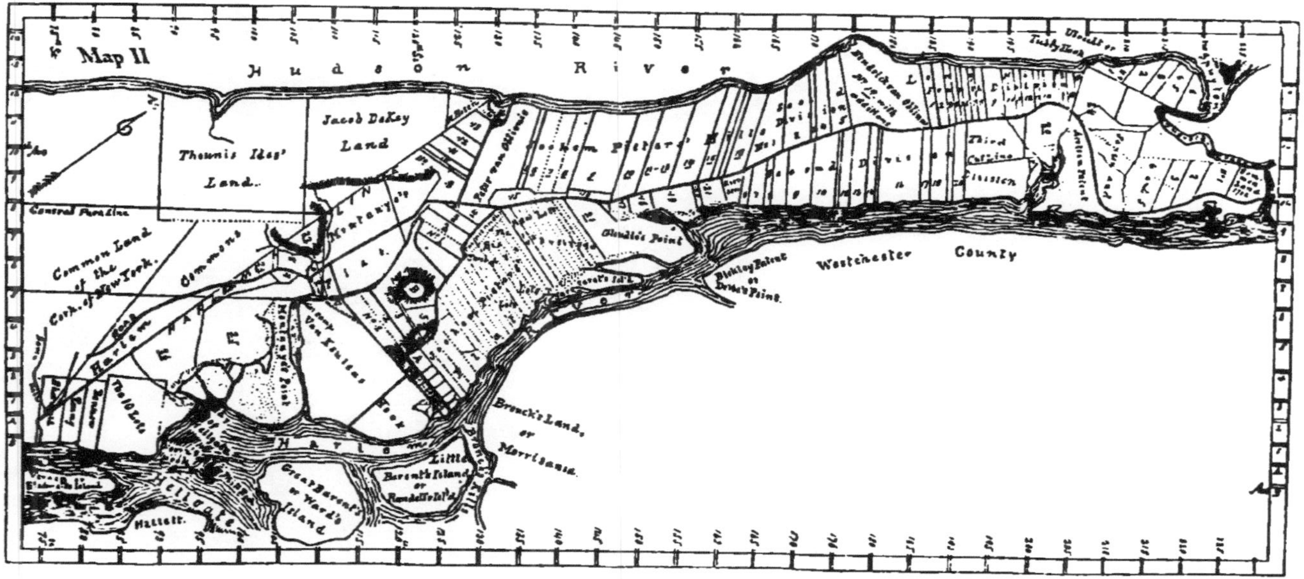

Map II
Hudson River
Jacob DeKey Land
Thounis Ides' Land
Common Land of the Corp. of New York
Harlem
Westchester County
Glendle's Point
Brock's Land, or Morrisania
Great Barent's or Ward's Island
Little Barent's Island or Randell's Isl'd
Hallett
The 10 Lots
Van Keulen's Hook
Montagne's Point
Third Division
Second Division
Tubby Hook
Archer Patent

Map III.

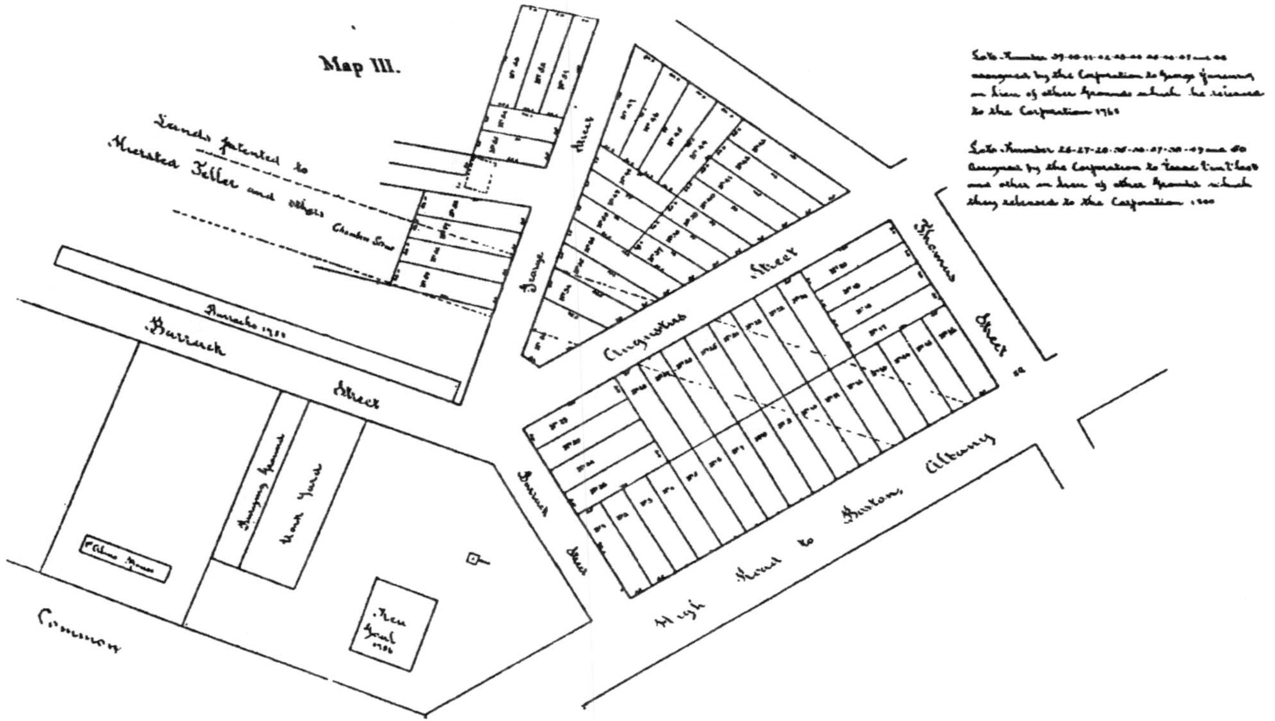
Barrack Street
George Street
Augustus Street
Thomas Street
Barrack Street
High Road to Boston Albany
Common

Map IV

Queen Street

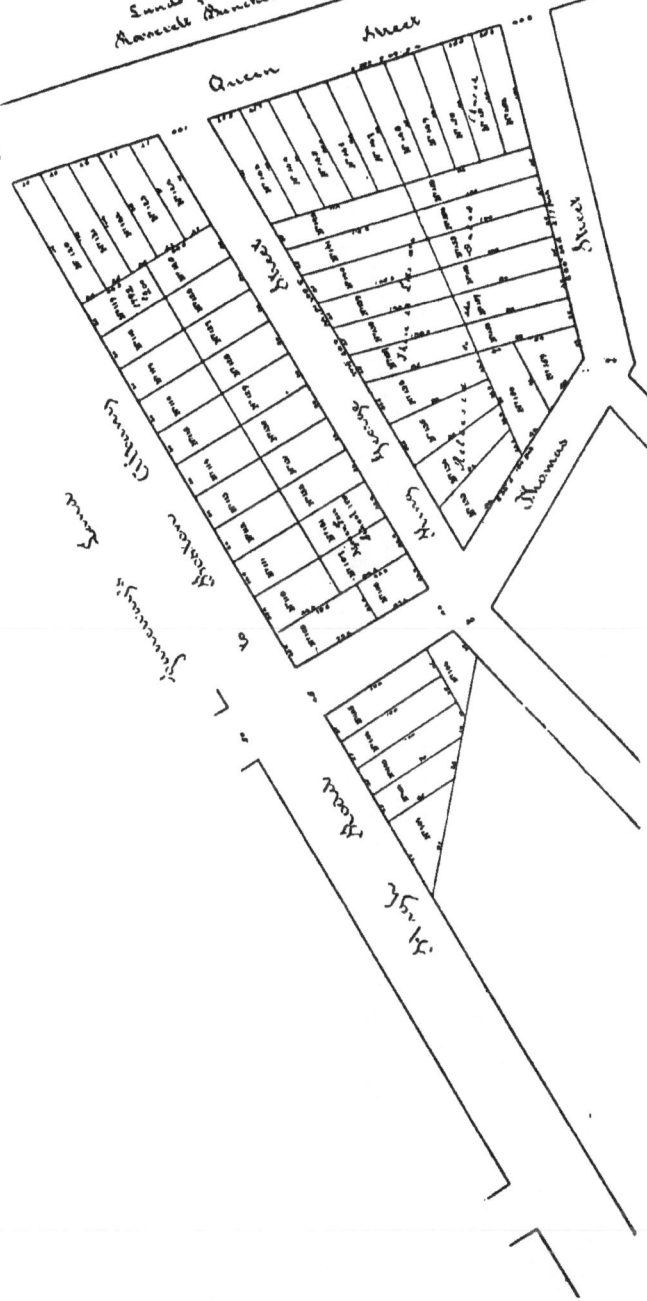

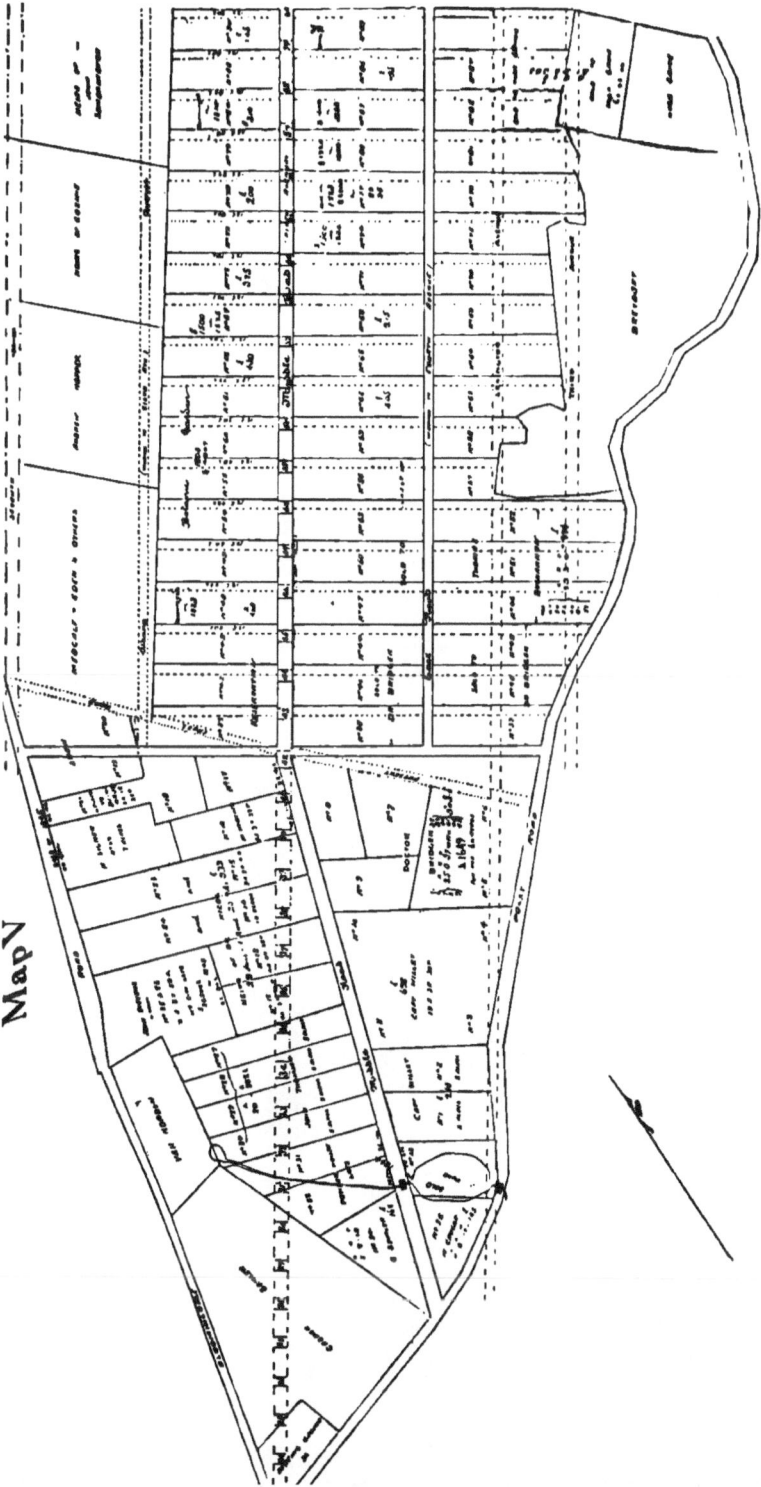
Map V

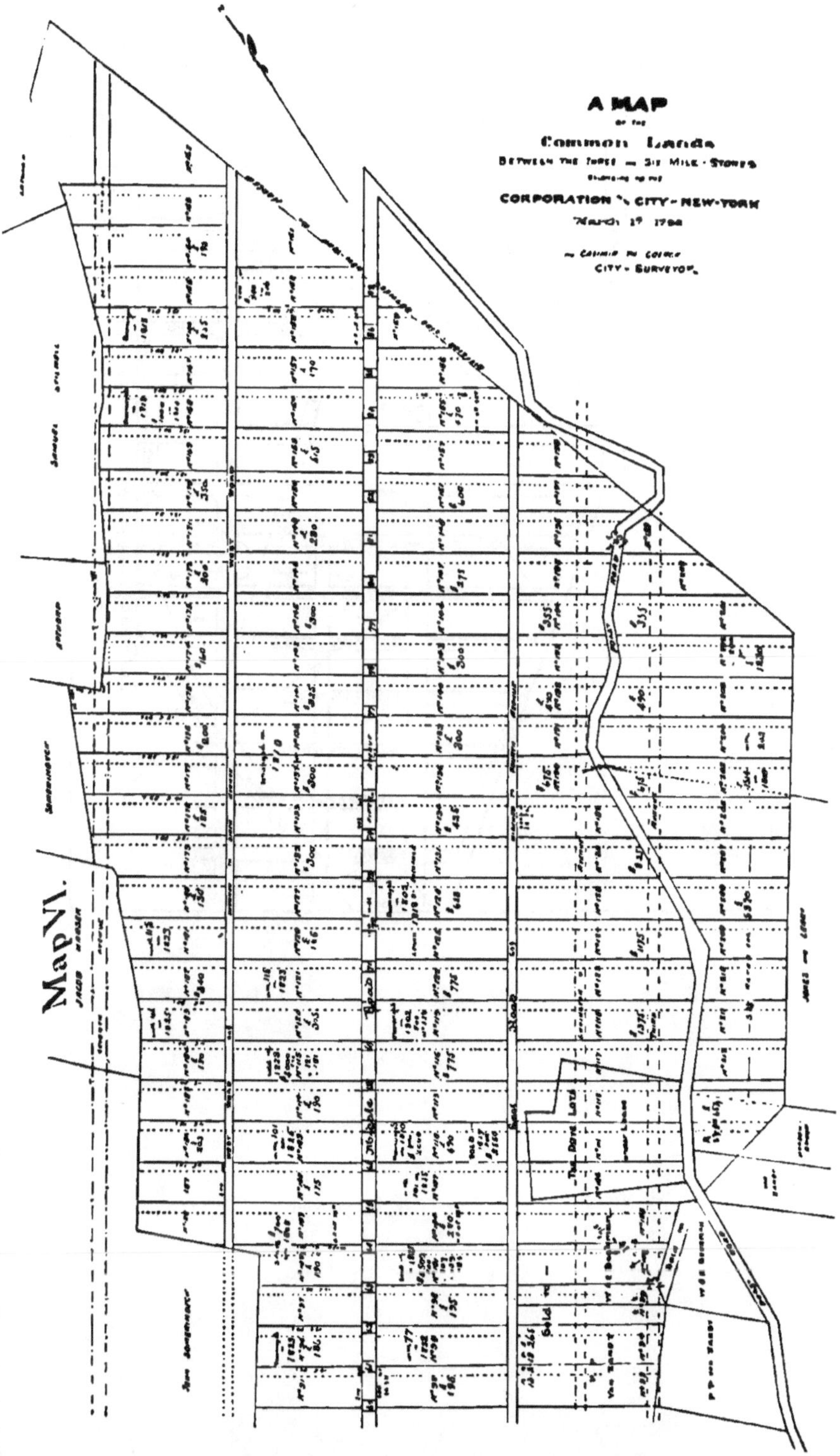

A MAP
of the
Common Lands
BETWEEN THE THREE — SIX MILE-STONES
belonging to the
CORPORATION of the CITY of NEW-YORK
March 19 1788

~ CASIMIR TH COLLES
CITY - SURVEYOR.

Map VI.

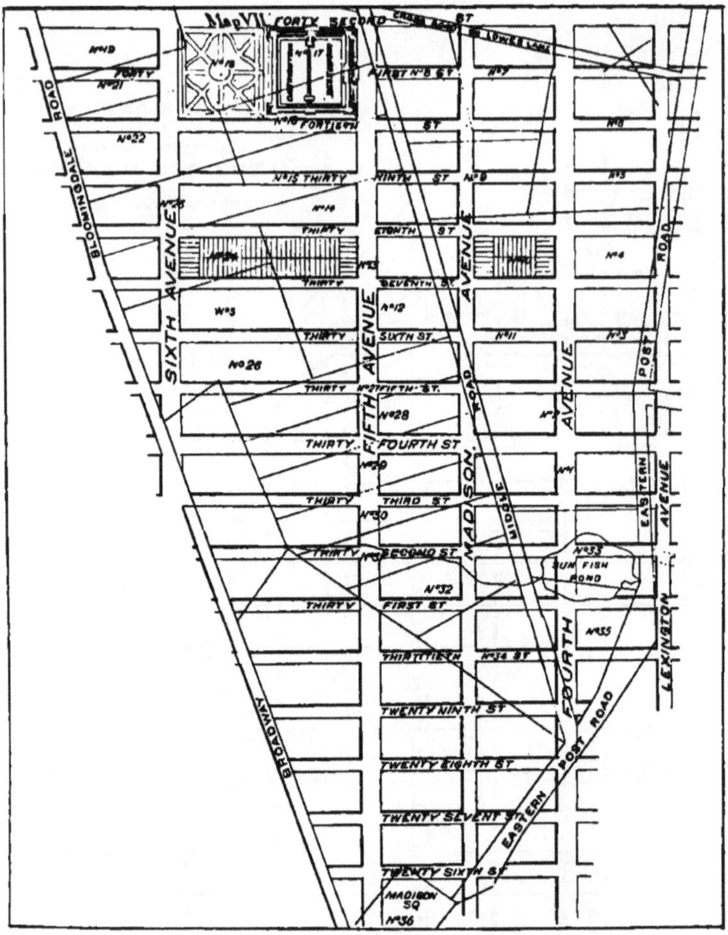

Map VII
FORTY SECOND ST
FORTY FIRST ST
THIRTY NINTH ST
THIRTY EIGHTH ST
THIRTY SEVENTH ST
THIRTY SIXTH ST
THIRTY FIFTH ST
THIRTY FOURTH ST
THIRTY THIRD ST
THIRTY SECOND ST
THIRTY FIRST ST
TWENTY NINTH ST
TWENTY EIGHTH ST
TWENTY SIXTH ST
BLOOMINGDALE ROAD
SIXTH AVENUE
FIFTH AVENUE
MADISON AVENUE
MIDDLE ROAD
FOURTH AVENUE
LEXINGTON AVENUE
EASTERN POST ROAD
BROADWAY
SUN FISH POND
MADISON SQ
No 21
No 22
No 26
No 28
No 30
No 32
No 33
No 35
No 36

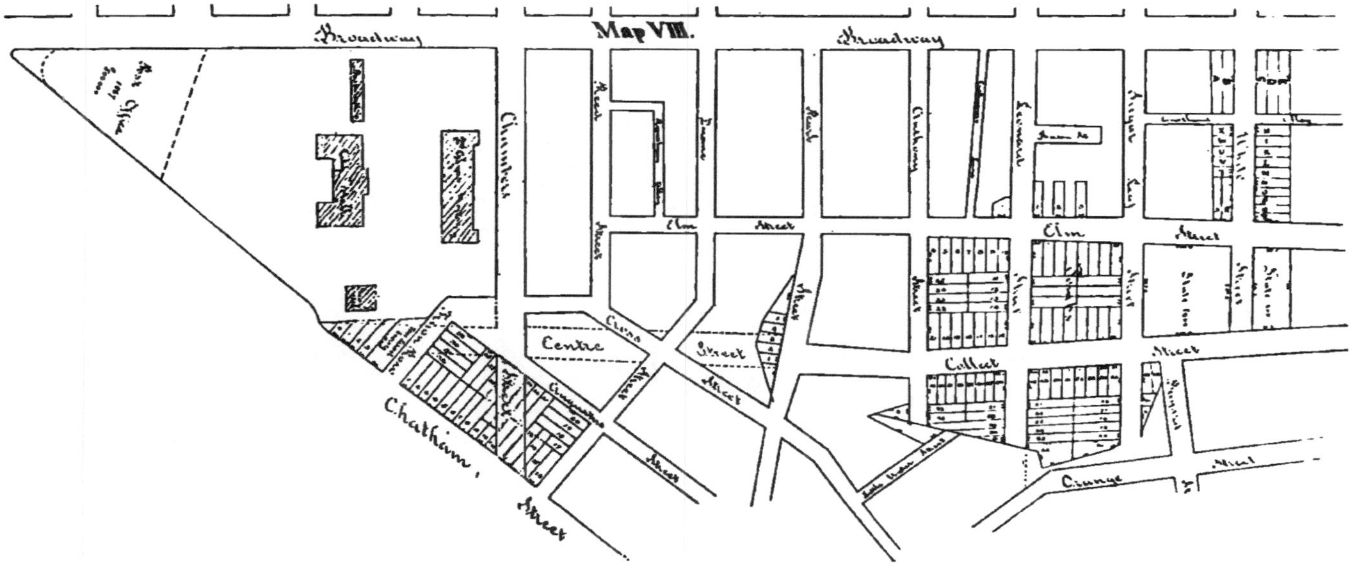

Map VIII.

State ...

White Street

State ...

Broadway

Augus Lane Street

Elm

Leonard Street

Collect

Anthony Street

Reade Street

Duane

Reade Street

Chambers

Broadway

Chatham Street

Centre

Post Office
1817

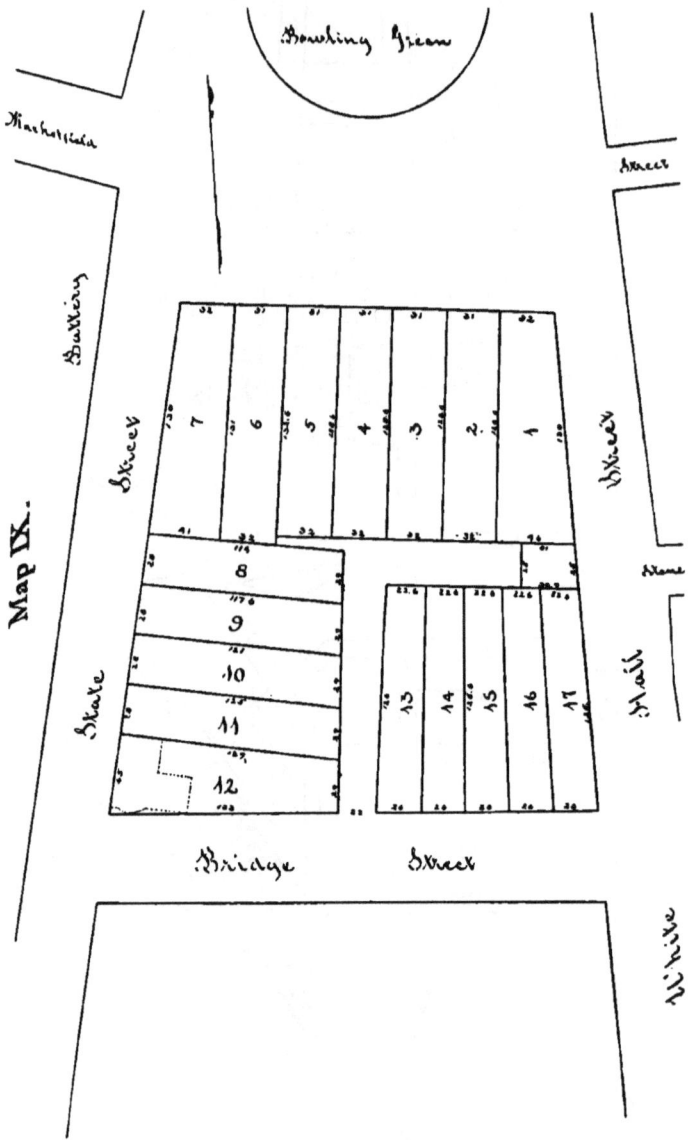

Map IX.

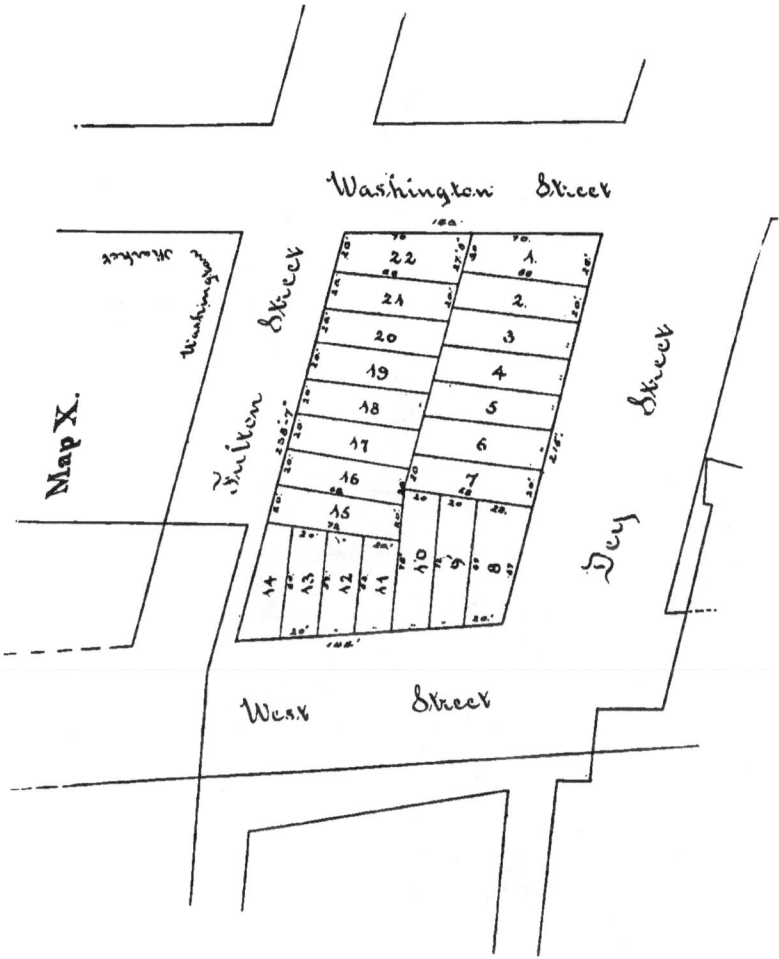

Washington Street

Map X.

Street

Washington

Fulton Street

Washington Street

22 1.
21 2.
20 3.
19 4.
18 5.
17 6.
16 7.
15
14 13 12 11 10 9 8

Dey Street

West Street

Map XI.

Greenwich Street

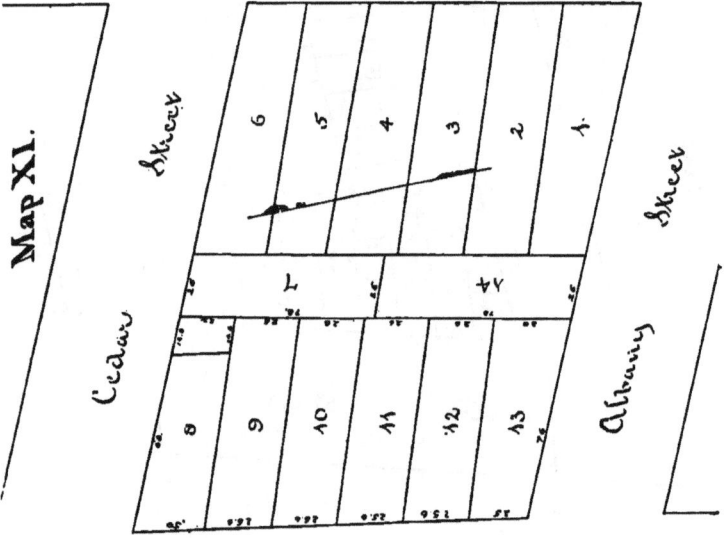

Cedar Street

6   5   4   3   2   1

7   14

8   9   10   11   12   13

Albany Street

Washington Street

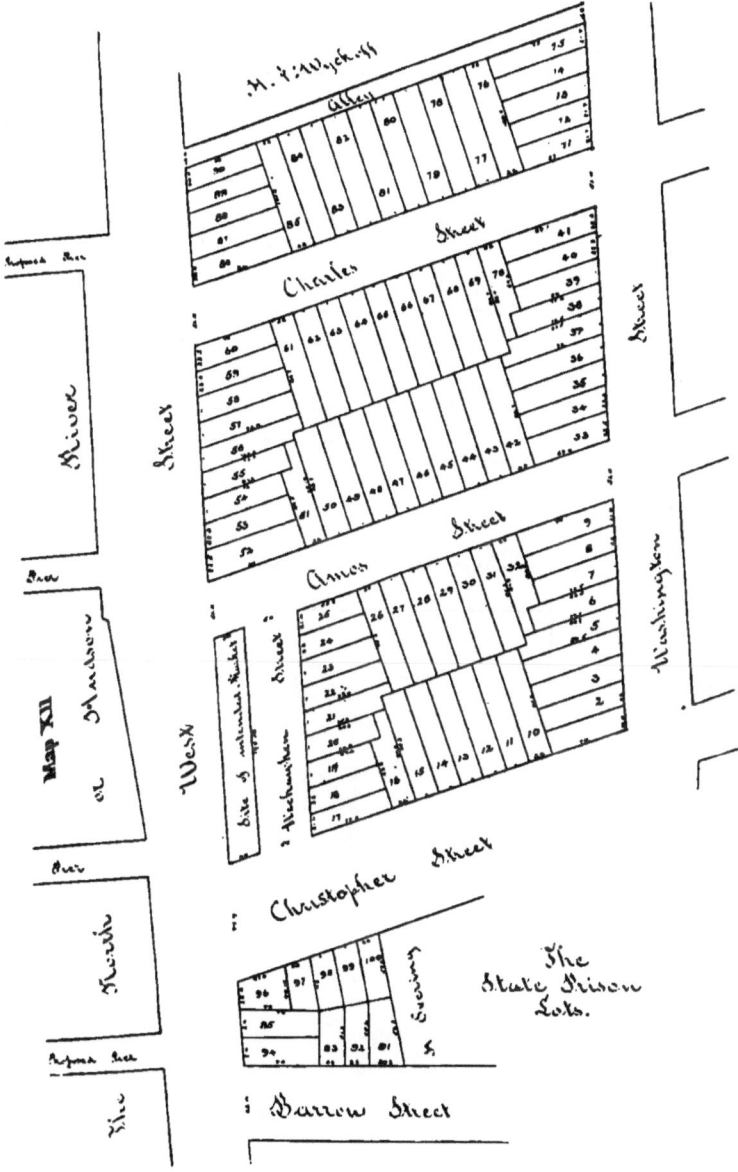

Map XII

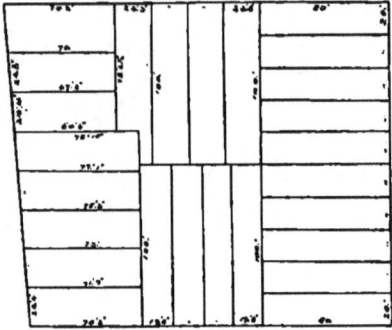

King Street

North River

West Street

Washington Street

Charlton Street

Map XIII.

Map XIV.

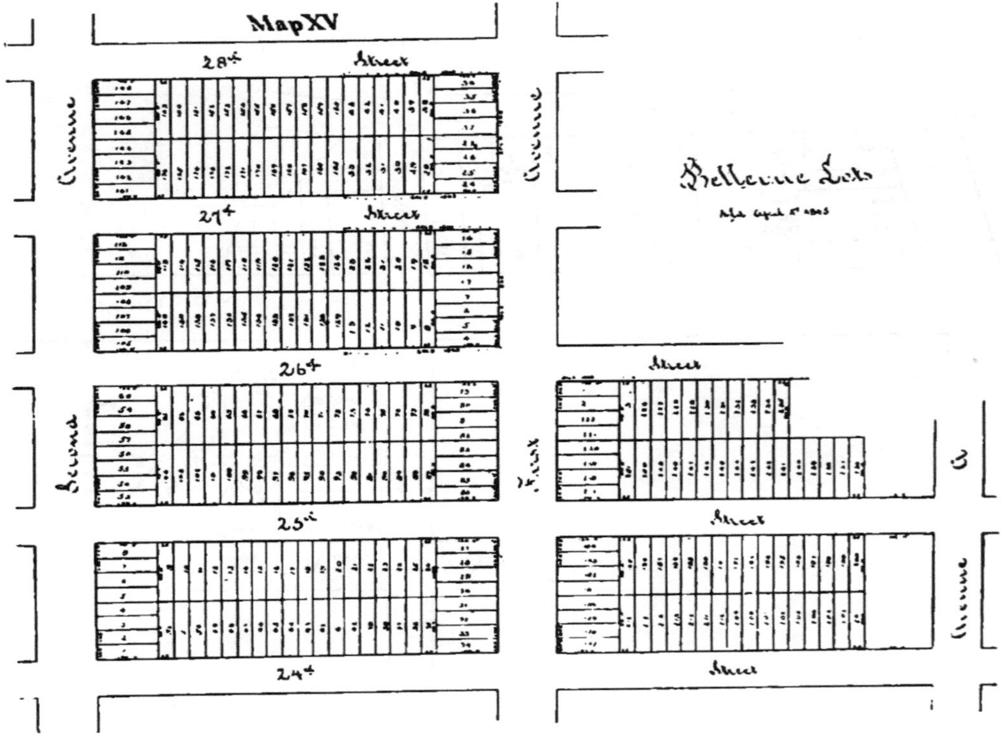
MapXV
28th Street
27th Street
26th Street
25th Street
24th Street
Avenue
Second
First
Street
Avenue
A
Bellevue Lots

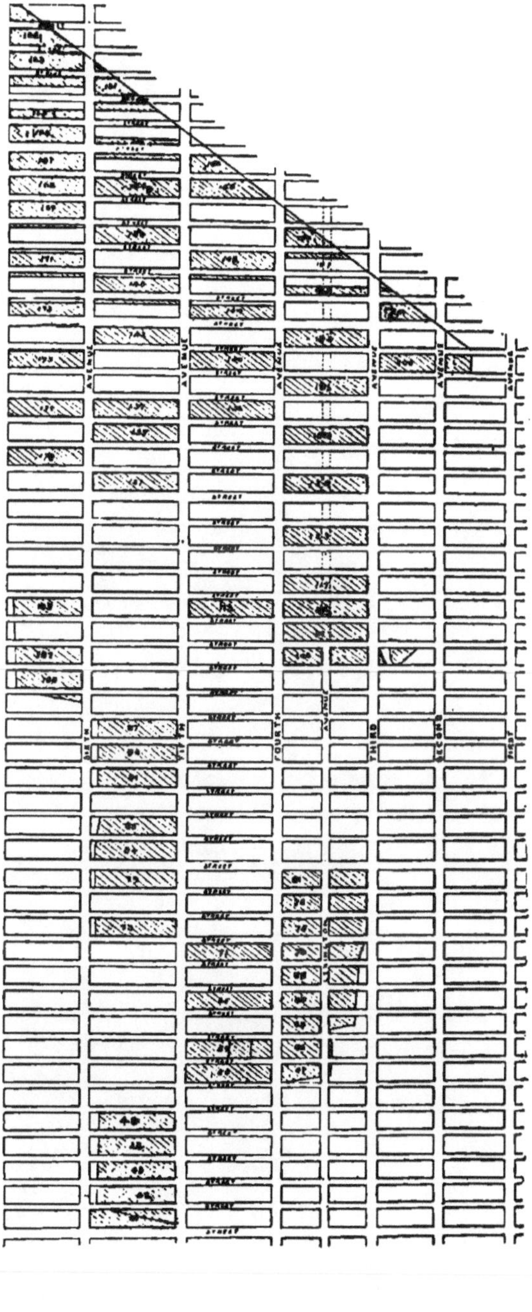

SIXTH
FIFTH
FOURTH
AVENUE
THIRD
SECOND
FIRST
STREET